Drifting Beneath the
"Red Duster"

Neil J. Morton

PNEUMA SPRINGS PUBLISHING UK

First Published in 2010 by:
Pneuma Springs Publishing

Pneuma Springs Publishing
A Subsidiary of Pneuma Springs Ltd.
7 Groveherst Road, Dartford Kent, DA1 5JD.
E: admin@pneumasprings.co.uk
W: www.pneumasprings.co.uk

A catalogue record for this book is available from the British Library.

Drifting Beneath the
the
"Red Duster"

Dedicated to
My mother, my sister, Fiona and Joy and my son Paul

Life's Big Decision

ONE DAY IN SCHOOL

Our new headmaster a Welshman, Mr Morris by name, had tipped the old curriculum on its head. In 1953 his predecessor, a man firmly entrenched in pre-war methods, retired. He took with him the shiny black jacket and pinstripe trousers that he habitually wore, with a stiff wing collar and a cravat fastened by a gold pin and all the other out-dated teaching methods and Edwardian stuffiness. Now we had more sports, even the assembly hall was turned into a gymnasium. We were given status as members of a house, and became proud of our athletic and sports abilities. The houses were named Garth, Kings, Staines, and Keyes, and the house emblems became part of our new school badge, quartered on a blue and gold shield. Even the name of this red brick pile changed for the better. We became Garth Secondary College. In later years Surrey County Council embraced co-education and my sister followed in my footsteps. Students were allowed to play with balls in the playground at recess—never allowed under the previous regime. The new man loved boxing and choir singing and I qualified to a minor degree in both disciplines. A wonderful South African music master, a smiling coloured man, tried to teach us, unsuccessfully, to read music, and played jazz and boogie woogie in the last minutes of the class provided we had been good boys. Soon with more emphasis on the Arts in general our minds began to flower, and a complete change took place: students whom as a matter of course "wagged it" as often as possible showed interest in the new curriculum.

In my case it was the written word and I received a great deal of encouragement, both at home and in class. I read, (devoured) books from

5

Biggles at age ten, then through the classics, plus *de Maupassant* and *Kafka, the risqué D.H. Lawrence*; in later years I even had a shot at the philosophers. My other great love was geography, and would pore over an atlas for hours. I had a cousin who as a steward in the Merchant Navy travelled far and wide; he enthralled me with his tales of New York, the Bahamas, and the Caribbean. I longed to see these exotic shores for myself.

One day, without warning the students of the senior class aged fourteen, had to go before the "head" for career planning. I awaited my turn knowing one thing for certain; there was no way that I would submit to the drab cycle of nine to five in factory or office, commuting through all weathers, like my mother who travelled for over an hour by bus and underground from Mitcham to the Aldwych five days a week to work as a telephonist at the Temple Bar exchange. My father had "shot through" soon after the war ended and my mother's country education and fine speaking voice had sustained us ever since.

In the headmaster's study the interview went something like this. 'Right Morton, I have your records before me and they provide a clear picture of your strengths and weaknesses. You know them as well as I do so we won't linger on math, wood and metal work, nature study, religious instruction, etc., and so it is sports, English, geography, and history that you prefer and are good at. Your voice has broken and you croak like a frog, so you are no longer in the choir and a crooner you'll never be! An apprenticeship as a tradesman, which is where most of my boys go is out, and definitely not a chorister. (He had a wicked sense of humour). What is it you would like to become when you leave us next year?'

'Well to be honest sir, my mother wants me to be a motor mechanic, but the idea of getting covered in grease and oil everyday does not appeal.'

'Your mother is a clever woman, there's a big future in the motor vehicle industry boy.'

Up until this moment only the vaguest idea of what I wanted to do with my life has struggled to the surface of my brain. Like most fourteen year olds, girls, clothes, football, girls, cricket, movies, girls, rock and roll and school holidays filled my waking hours. Miraculously, words from somewhere down in the depths of my subconscious came tumbling out;

'I want to join the Merchant Navy sir.'

'What,' the good man cried, 'that is the waste of a good brain, you don't have the math for navigation and you said yourself engineering is too messy so what is left?'

'Steward Sir, just like my cousin Terry.'

The silence was deafening.

That night I broke the news to the family. Following a stunned silence my sister, who shared a room with another female cousin, jumped up and cried,

'Can I have his room mum?'

The remainder of my school year was spent waiting on the teachers' tables in the canteen, and on leaving a further twelve months in two of London's finest West End hotels, The Hyde Park, and The Howard. The Howard was in Surrey St; opposite Australia House, close to the Inns of Court in Fleet Street and the Temple. The clientele of The Howard comprised for the most part members of the legal profession and journalists. The more up market Hyde Park had the most enormous kitchens way down in the bowls of the earth. At meal times scores of commis waiters, including the author, laboured like ants climbing steep staircases toting huge circular trays laden with silver salvers filled with delicious food, the aromas of which would make my stomach growl.

On one spectacular evening I was selected to serve at the table of Her Majesty, and Prince Phillip. Although I must admit I only held tureen and salver for our Maitre D'hotel to actually place the delicacies on the royal plates. Needless to say this training was to stand me in good stead in years to come.

Shortly after this event I went to Leadenhall Street and joined the Merchant Service. Documentation soon followed as in the mid 1950s lads like me were in short supply to man the vessels that at that time comprised the largest merchant fleet in the world.

T.S. Vindicatrix, (training ship) a legend to seafarers who trained aboard her, was to be my home for six weeks; 70,000 boys passed through this venerable vessel learning to be deckhands or stewards. Here we learned the right way to clean a cabin, make a bunk, peel a spud, lay a table, polish silverware, sail a lifeboat, learned that left was Port, and right was Starboard. On completion we were issued with a basic and scratchy navy blue serge uniform, complete with Merchant Navy shoulder flashes and our badges of proficiency sewn on the sleeves. We were also issued with two blue and white striped heavy cotton work shirts, known for some obscure reason as "piss jackets", and then sent to various ships at ports all around the British Isles.

What followed I could never have gleaned from any book. The life I had chosen was to be rich and full. Adventure fell at my wandering feet like manna from on high. I trust you will enjoy reading about some of the amazing escapades that befell a green and romantic lad from the dreary suburbs of South London.

Today I sit in my backyard in a suburb of Melbourne, about a mile from a crescent of golden beach that curves in a clean sweep for thirty miles to our city centre. The early spring sun shoots sparks of golden light off the palms and bamboos that I have planted on the fence line. A south westerly breeze stirs the branches of a giant gum tree that must be over one hundred years old casting dancing shadows on the tile roof of my home and the azure surface of the pool. Our old Boxer dog Misty lies in the shade her grey muzzle twitching; a dog barks up the street, her ears flick and she looks up at me and tells me not to worry it's just that stupid Shiatsu.

My wife Joy calls from the kitchen, 'would you like your drink freshened?' What follows is all about the road, or should I say the shipping lanes that carried me here.

Melbourne 2008.

Part One
BRAZIL

Dismay; total and utter, caused me to drop my suitcase in disgust at the sight of the ship that the Shipping Federation had sent me to join. The new leather bag splashed rain water from a murky puddle ruining the shine on my new shoes and splattering the cuffs of my trousers. Three weeks ago I had signed off from a smart Cunarder out of King George V dock in the Pool of London, and having seen enough of East Coast USA, I had taken a short leave, and then reported to the offices of the Federation of British Seamen, known as the "pool," looking for work. They sent me to this old tub sailing to Brazil for a three or four month run. The filthy old bucket looked as if she would have difficulty steaming out of the docking basin into the Thames and I wondered if she would make it past the Azores. I had about three quid and some silver left from my last pay off, otherwise I would have gone back to the "pool" and told them to forget it.

Lying very low against the gritty concrete quayside under an early winter sky, the old Liberty ship painted in flaking black and beige, with rust streaking from the hawsehole and gunnels, looked in need of a dry dock and a good going over, or the salvage yard. Built in Portland Oregon during the war years of 1940-44 vessels of this vintage were churned out at a record rate. This was mainly due to the USA's mass production method of welding the steel plates together instead of the traditional laborious riveting. The Marshal Plan, America's helping hand to a beleaguered Britain, paid for these vessels and they carried precious cargos across the U-Boat infested waters of the North Atlantic and brought new life to an embattled Europe. As a result, the life expectancy of these vessels was minimal. Somehow this ship, bearing the legend *S.S. Barranca*, in scaly white letters across her stern, had survived until 1956. I was to learn at a later date the name of the old scow meant gully or small ravine in Portuguese. The owners, Royal Mail, plied the Spanish and South American coast and many of the company's ships had Spanish or Portuguese names.

Utilitarian to the extreme her lines were basically ugly. Single decked with bridge and accommodation amidships and a small poop deck aft, this old ship was to be my home for the foreseeable future. October showers and a cold wind clawed at my clothes and gear as I looked about me at the dockers huddled under their flat caps and donkey jackets. I heard the rattle and screech of winches and cranes as she discharged cargo; glimpsed oil spills, rainbow hued, in the puddles caused by the rain sheeting off the shed roofs. Hefting my suitcase in one hand and my old Imperial portable typewriter in its scuffed leather case, I climbed aboard using the clanking, virtually horizontal gangway at the head of which a burly, red-haired seaman, leaning casually against the side asked in a broad Scots accent, 'Hold up there son what would you be looking for?'

'Joining as steward's boy,' I replied.

'You'll want the Chief then?'

I stood on the still vibrating gangway the rain soaking my hair and running down the back of my shirt collar, which did not improve my mood. I took in the broad shoulders that strained the seams of a washed out blue pea jacket, the weather-beaten face with the tiny red lines of grog indulgence and the steady judgemental brown eyes and decided not give him a smart answer.

After our brief exchange he turned and walked to an open port hole and bellowed,

'Hey Chiefie, there's a wee laddie here looking for you. By the look of him he'll need plenty of your porridge.'

Now whereas I was on the skinny side, I stood six feet tall, and at the age of seventeen going on eighteen, had plenty of time to fill out and definitely not on burgoo. Giving him a look which I hoped would nip the wee laddie stuff in the bud, I strolled to the nearest entry and stepping over the storm water coaming swung my bags in and nearly whacked a short, portly, balding man with the old Imperial. 'Careful son, have you got a licence for that thing?'

From his smart navy blue uniform and gold rings, I knew him to be my new boss.

'Sorry sir, Tom Morgan reporting for duty.'

'Well now Mr Morgan, you'll be our pantry boy. My name is Cassidy, mister to you or chief, I don't mind which.'

His immaculate appearance, from highly polished shoes to glowing newly shaved jaws in a round ruddy face reassured me that this vessel was not entirely without hope. With an accent decidedly dockside Liverpool he stated, 'thank the Lord you're not a first tripper. Follow me and we'll get your gear stowed.'

I followed him down a gloomy alleyway painted dreary beige with a black painted hand rail running down the inner bulkhead, something to grab onto in heavy seas. The deck head, obscured in a tangle of pipes smelled faintly of roach powder. My bags thumped in the narrow space echoing off the steel passageway. As we progressed further, aft I noticed an aromatic, spicy whiff wafting through the enclosed air combating the usual smell of oil, sweaty socks, and wet weather gear. Abruptly we turned a corner amidships and came upon the galley, inside which three figures in white cotton jackets and blue checked cooks' trousers turned to stare at the new arrival. The colour of their ebony skin, highlighted by the snowy jackets, appeared to have been polished to a high degree.

'Hey Chester!' the chief called, and a lad of about my own age stepped forward.

'Yes boss,' he acknowledged the shout.

'Take Morgan here to your berth, and double back quick smart.'

'I'm on my way, Mr Cassidy.'

Chester scuttled ahead of me to the starboard alleyway and threw open the door of a small cabin which contained two bunks. Everything was steel, even the bunks were built from lead coloured piping bolted to the deck. The deck head contained the usual a tangle of steel encased conduit running from bulkhead to bulkhead, with drainage pipes gurgling. A grey painted metal locker was to serve as my wardrobe. A single porthole with a heavy deadlight suspended on a hook, let in the watery grey light of a gloomy UK season which I would be glad to kiss goodbye. A thin cotton tick mattress lay folded beside a pillow, one grey blanket, and a Board of Trade counterpaign.

'Chester, they do better in Wormwood Scrubs than this,' I stated in disgust.

Chester, a roly-poly individual with fat cheeks, smiled from ear to ear revealing huge white teeth and gestured to the left hand bunk which ran amidships on the forward bulkhead,

'How come you know that man, you been inside? Chuck 'em on there mate, when old 'Hopalong' says double he means it.'

Back at the galley door the chief beckoned me around an adjacent corner into a bibby alleyway and led me into an area of about eight feet by six feet, which contained a sink piled high with dirty cups, saucers, plates and cutlery. 'This is your station Morgan, there's an apron somewhere, look lively and clean this lot up and report to Wang the saloon steward when it's done.' This *lot* looked like it had been there for a week.

'Strewth!' I muttered under my breath, talk about welcome aboard.

Fortunately for yours truly I had spent the last year or so doing the same thing, only in much more salubrious surroundings. An hour later with soaking wet shirtsleeves, I stuck my head through a hatch above the hot press that led onto the officers' dining saloon. A diminutive Oriental was polishing tumblers and setting them on the three round tables that seated eight officers apiece at meal times, each table boasted white tablecloths, resplendent with heavy silver cutlery, the company logo etched into the handle of each knife, fork, and spoon.

'Oi!' he yelled, 'what do you think you're staring at mate?'

The word think came out as 'fink', so I knew I had a fellow Londoner to work with.

'Are you Wang?' as if I didn't know.

'No, I'm Sophia Loren, if you're the new pantry boy, get your backside in here and help with these glasses.'

This man was dressed in a starched white mess jacket; some of the old soup stains crusted deep in the weave fastened tightly at the neck, black trousers and spit shined black shoes. His face looked as if someone had hit it with a cricket bat it was so flat, the teeth were cracked and yellow. He gave me a clean glass cloth and disappeared through a heavy timber door leaving me with around twenty tumblers to polish and set on the tables. Ten minutes later he reappeared accompanied by a tall thin Negro with a highly polished bald head edged around with a fringe of grey peppercorn hair.

'This here is Monty he's the Captains steward and also does the officers' quarters. I do the engineers, we both serve on these three tables at meal times and you do as you're told OK?'

Monty was at least six feet four inches tall, stooped over with bones as thin as twigs; he had a permanently lost expression on his equine face. The lugubrious features rarely smiled, but when it did, teeth like a Derby winner overflowed his thick lips. I glanced at a large brass clock on the bulkhead above a mahogany sideboard; it read fifteen minutes past eleven. Lunch would be served from noon, in two sittings. Above this elegant furniture was a painting of a distant sunny plain, presumably in Portugal or Spain, the vibrant colours of which appeared to illuminate and give warmth to this handsome eatery obviously refitted for officer comforts at some time after 1945.

The chief stuck his grinning face around the door. 'How's it going son, you seem to have the knack, check out the menu and I'll see you later. Oh, see the 2nd steward and draw your bed linen.' I found the 2nd in his single berth cabin next door to that of the chief steward, another man of colour he was poring over a large ledger making notes in pencil. On my request he reluctantly pushed back his chair grabbed a bunch of keys and led me below deck to the storage area. This guy had a head as round as a cannonball in the middle of which a small turned up nose battled to hold up a pair of specs that continually slipped causing him to brush them up again in a nervous tic. His big belly and round bum signalled plenty of good eating, maybe this ship was a good feeder to make up for the lack of charm. Everything appertaining to the issue of catering and cleaning stores fell to this man. This below decks alleyway also contained the galley storeroom and deep freeze locker.

He turned at a heavy door the key, poised weighing me up through the thumb smeared specs, 'My name is Charlie and you get a linen change fortnightly, you draw stores for the pantry once a week on Tuesday at 1000 hours so make sure you get it right OK? Do not come to me at any other time 'cause all you'll get is a flea in the ear, understand?'

Shanghaied on this wretched scow with a crew full of odd balls was all I needed. In the cabin I hung my good suit in the tin locker and threw my uniform on the bunk. Uniform ha, it wasn't much; two pairs of heavy navy blue serge trousers, two pairs of well washed and faded jeans, some underwear, three white mess jackets and two heavy cotton blue striped blouse style shirts known for some arcane reason as "piss jackets", that were worn over a T-shirt. Reporting to the chief's office ten minutes later dressed in jeans and T-shirt I presented him with my discharge book, which he would keep in the ship's safe until the voyage ended. Hopefully the voyage, in what to my mind were "romantic places", would make up for the cheerless surrounds. The pantry where I was to spend hours of drudgery for which I received the princely sum of eleven pounds sterling a month, comprised of a sink, a bain-marie with hot press beneath, a copper urn for making coffee, and some scrubbed wooden drying racks for plates mounted on the bulkhead. Mercifully there was a porthole at eye level immediately over the sink through which I could see the bustle of dockers and deck hands loading cargo. A tangle of mobile cranes which ran on steel tracks lifted cargo into *Barranca's* waiting holds.

A deep mellifluous voice with a strange twang interrupted my reverie. 'Hey don't stand there daydreaming son, come along to the galley for the soup, it goes in the bain-marie. Make sure you have plenty of soup bowls in the warmer. What's your name son?'

Turning, I saw a beaming Negro wiping his chubby hands on a white apron that almost covered his feet. At last, a bit of civility, I took the offered hand with a deep sense of relief.

'Tom, Tom Morgan.'

'Morgan, we is all from Jamaica in the galley and don't take kindly to that name unless it be on a bottle of rum. I am Winston, chief cook.' This was stated with another chuckle. 'Come on, we have nice minestrone for you down here. The cooks serve all the courses from the hot shelf to the two stewards, your job is to ladle out the soup on request and make the coffee and tea. How you feel about being the only white man among all us all?'

14

'Doesn't worry me,' I offered with a shrug, although I confessed to myself I could just as easily have walked away. Only time would tell, it also explained 'Hopalong's' ghoulish amusement as he was the only other 'white man' in the catering department.

So that was the way it went, three meals a day, plus suppers for the watch keepers, day after day for a week, until the routine became automatic; as was the scrubbing and cleaning of the pantry and saloon, plus cleaning the chief's office and cabin. In my mind I began to call the chief a 'Scouse git', he took an egg and bacon sandwich and fresh brewed coffee every morning at 0700, yours truly to oblige.

The wonderful aromas that I had observed on my first day were generated by the spices that Winston and Ambrose, his reclusive assistant, used in the curries and sauces, that were very popular with all hands. I could see that Monty was the eldest among us he shuffled around on huge outward splayed feet, and constantly held the small of his back after bending to serve at table. He was kind and helpful to me in those early days, unlike Wang who liked to bully, even though there was barely two pennyworth of him.

Chester was a scamp, a bouncy ball of happiness, content with his lot; he adored the second cook Ambrose, whom on closer inspection proved to be a mix of black and white blood. Tall and strong of build, with regular, almost European features, he had hazel eyes softening to green, very disconcerting when one met his full unblinking gaze. In contrast to the chief he prepared the food with a quiet efficiency of motion, whilst Winston banged and clattered pots and even threw them when vexed.

Fully stored and loaded we sailed under the dismal skies of a still wet winter hopefully to sunnier climes across the Atlantic, next stop Brazil. On the way I became firm friends with my shipmates in the galley. These Jamaican born Brits enjoyed life to the full. Always happy, their transistor radio tuned to Latin and Caribbean stations that churned out rhythms that set the toes tapping and the fingers beating on any available surface. Chester was a "dab hand" on an up turned saucepan, his fingers flew, and his beaming smiles created an ambience of goodwill. Ambrose enjoyed in his own quiet way. All the stewards were a miserable bunch. I therefore spent all my free time in the company of the galley staff. My grandmother on my mother's side had a large dollop of Spanish blood in her veins and I found the Latin rhythms much to my liking. The life boat drills and captains rounds, Wednesday and Sunday, broke up the monotony of the crossing via the Azores and Curacao for bunkering.

$\cdots$

Our first port of call was Recife way up on the north coast. The harbour facilities that greeted my excited eager eyes were a shade disappointing, just a small timber constructed wharf capable of containing only two ships at a time. The township, scattered over a few acres, and set against a backdrop of verdant vegetation, basked in brilliant sunshine. A canopy of green threatened to envelope the flimsy timber shacks I could see on the outer perimeter. A handful of brick and stone buildings marked the main thoroughfare; they included the customs house, and a court house complete with jail. Both available berths were occupied so we dropped anchor within hailing distance of an enormous American freighter, also at anchor.

That night we sat on the canvas covered cargo holds looking at the stars in an incredibly clear sky, swapping yarns the way sailors do and looking forward to a run ashore. Among us the deckhands and engine room firemen off watch sat spinning tall stories, mostly concerned with previous voyages, the girls and the booze. I sat with the cooks and stewards sipping cocoa and listening. This seeming segregation was totally innocent of malice, it was just the way it traditionally had been and most likely still is. I have sailed on ships of all sizes from this bucket up to a fresh off the shipyards "maiden voyager," and an unspoken rule seems to separate the various ships' departments, apart from the sensible polite courtesy of men in an enclosed environment, we rarely mix socially. With my eighteenth birthday coming up in a few weeks I listened avidly to every colourful word which was most educational.

Early next day, while the sun was a faint golden glow in the east and there was a fresh breeze of the mainland heavy with exotic spicy aromas, one of the ships, a Panamanian, sailed with the tide and the pilot took us into a bustling dockside. Wharfies clad in tattered but clean looking shorts and tee shirts ran up and down the heavy timber planks of the wharf yelling instructions to one another as aided by a little green painted tug we were nudged into our berth.

'Tonight we are going to have some fun,' stated Chester as he leaned over the side with me studying the activity.

'Oh no you don't,' came the Liverpudlian drawl from behind us, of course it was the Chief. 'You do not go ashore anywhere in Brazil without an adult to accompany you. The pair of you are minors in my care and those are the regulations until you are eighteen.'

This rule had never cropped up on my previous two voyages to the States, so I wondered if Brazil was dangerous or just full of temptation and traps for 'wet behind the ears lads'.

'Why don't you take us chief, you must know this place pretty good?'

'No way boys, I'm saving all my money for Rio.'

It was Ambrose in his quiet matter of fact way that offered to escort Chester and I ashore that evening. After the heat, bustle, and clamour of a ship discharging cargo, the peace and quiet of a short stroll into town was balm to my over-stimulated curiosity.

Around us, as the air cooled in the early evening dusk, the Brasileiros moved with a solemn grace each with a smile and a murmured greeting. Ambrose, normally a silent soul, replied in the same smooth tones as we walked, glancing from side to side at the shops and cafes. We paused at a small café where teenage kids danced to Latin rhythms from a loud thumping jukebox. We each had a cold bottle of Coca-Cola the dew running down frosty sides and a sweet sticky pastry and then decided to go to the one and only cinema. The posters outside declared that Alan Ladd was showing in the classic western *Shane*. The theatre was an open-air building with long rows of canvas seating just like giant elongated deck chairs. The seating was deep and comfortable where we all sat cheek by jowl. Every time someone moved the whole canvas shook like a sail in the wind. The American actors, speaking English with a western drawl, translated into Portuguese subtitles at the bottom of the screen, caused Chester and I to chuckle quietly together during the film, which I have always thought much over-rated.

We came out at around nine thirty, after three and a bit weeks at sea with plenty of sleep, the thought of going back aboard did not appeal. Ambrose looked at our expectant young faces, 'Do you reckon you can handle a cold beer?'

'You're the boss Ambrose, 'we declared in unison.

'Just beer, and one is all you get, and only one is that understood?'

17

Little did he know that I was accustomed to downing a pint or two in the Nags Head at the Fair Green in my home town?

Ambrose led us off the main drag and down a side street, an alley really, sand crunched beneath our feet. Lighting such as it was came from the shuttered windows of timber and tar paper shacks with ludicrous names like Great Southern Tavern and Tropicana Café. Street traders stared as we passed, calling from the shadows:

'Hey Mac, you wanna buy a good watch, very cheap?'

'Hello Johnny, you wanna good time?'

A cart lit by a kerosene lamp on which a small cauldron bubbled and spat offered deep fried squid and shrimp, in the background the sounds of strummed guitars, very romantic.

The humid night pushed down, a trickle of sweat searched for my right eye. The sky was almost totally dark, the people in the gloom almost invisible. The bulk of Ambrose was reassuring. I became aware of the steadily growing sound of Elvis Presley banging out *Blue Suede Shoes* as we approached a saloon better illuminated than the others. My blood quickened, above the door written in red and blue light globes were the legend *Texas Bar*.

Inside, half of *Barranca's* crew sat firmly ensconced with beers and shot glasses of rum at hand, they joined in the chorus with raucous abandon. Amidst the sweaty atmosphere, redolent with tobacco and alcohol fumes, our red haired bosun Angus by name, sat with two other sturdy looking members of the deck department, they looked sun tanned and tough in a room of tough looking characters. The thin cotton shirt plastered with sweat on Angus's sturdy frame looked about to burst over his chest.

'Hey Ambrose get over here,' he called 'let me buy you a beer, and the two laddies with you.'

'Thanks bosun, but we are just having the one and then away.' The two laddies heartily agreed.

'Rubbish, you look after my lads and it's time your friends put hair on their chests.'

He stood with a push on the table, already liberally scattered with empty bottles and cigarette butts, causing more grog to spill into an already large puddle. Striding to the bar he crunched through discarded peanut shells that littered the floor, apparently bowls of these nuts in their shells came free with the drinks. Thumping the bar he called for three Brahma Chops. Mystified, I watched as three long necked bottles with condensation running frostily down the sides appeared on the bar, it turned out that this was the brand name of the brew. Elvis had just got started on *Jailhouse Rock* and the crew all joined in the chorus. I took a sip from the neck of the cold lager and all the lights went out.

'What the heck!' exclaimed Ambrose?

Catcalls, whistles, stamping feet and curses, rent the blackness. Suddenly there came a rustle of a silk like fabric, accompanied by the stink of sweat and cheap perfume and a soft bundle sat on my knees placing an arm around my neck, a voice murmured,

'Hello Johnny,' it breathed in my ear whilst grasping my sex beneath the table.

Startled, I stood bolt upright, the lights came back on, at my feet a plump and pretty girl howled derision up at me. Half the crew had done the same thing and chaos reigned. What with the screams of the discarded business girls lying amongst the peanut shells, the roar of laughter from the men, we did not notice the arrival of half a dozen tanned, burly, crew-cut sailors from the American freighter. They wore drill shirts tucked into Levi 101s and one or two wore cowboy boots.

'Hey! You Limeys,' one of them yelled, 'if you don't want those girls send 'em over here.'

'Go get your own pussy, Yank,' yelled Angus. Why do natural allies resent one another so much?

'Looks like you guys and boys,' this one fellow with a square head sporting a crew cut stared at Chester and me, 'never did learn how to handle ladies, then maybe you don't need to board that bucket being Limeys and all.'

The atmosphere changed in the blink of an eye. A few seconds of electric silence, and then the first glass flew followed by boots and fists, tables were upturned and chairs skidded madly across the littered floor. I thought I was back in the western saloon with a scrawny Alan Ladd punching his way through the villains, until a large glass ashtray hit me full on the nose and I went down in the filth. Ambrose picked me up and grabbing Chester by the arm charged out of there. It must have taken all of thirty seconds, thirty seconds that changed the shape of my nose.

Back aboard the ship, our radio officer, who doubled as ship's doctor, shoved me into the poop deck cabin laughingly called a hospital, and stuffed cotton wool up my nostrils and pushed my nose roughly back into shape. Whilst still in the throes of agony and remorse, Mr Cassidy, his face lit with false concern, told me in no uncertain terms that I was confined to the ship. Ambrose received a severe dressing down from the skipper for taking us to the roughest bar in town.

· · · · ·

Whilst resting in the quiet hospital bunk I looked back at the voyage so far. A few days earlier we had stopped to take on oil and mail at the small island of Curacao in the Caribbean. At daybreak one morning I had climbed a rocky outcrop dotted here and there with twisted scrubby trees and a waxlike deep green plant. Tiny tendrils and weblike roots held these persistent enduring plants in place and despite nature's punishing onslaughts, they survived.

Having heaved myself up the last few feet I stood on a huge boulder that had been scoured over eons of time by hurricane winds, baking sunlight, flying salt spray and tropical downpours. The day was serene about me, the sky a vast dome of cloudless blue, the turquoise ocean painted in scintillating shades of green and deepening hues of aqua sparkled beneath my feet. The perfect sky and the horizon melted into one seamless scene of story book beauty. The clean ozone layer was sucked deep into my lungs; the very sharpness of the air jolted me into the remembrance of a special day when my headmaster had taken me to his study to ask about my plans for a career. 'I will go to sea sir.'

'What!' that worthy gentleman had exclaimed, 'you will waste a good brain.'

'That is my choice sir, not for me the nine 'til five routine;' I was determined to leave the grime and often grim London suburbs, let the poor bastards who had no choice have it.

In the clear still air the vista before me was smudged by the ugly bulk of *Barranca* moored at the end of a long jetty taking on oil for her ancient engines. A tendril of oily smoke feathered upward from the galley exhaust. Maybe it was the intoxicating romance of the Caribbean, for the history of these islands tugged at my subconscious, tall ships with canvas billowing before the trade winds. Somehow the ugliness of *Barranca* had softened. After all she was my conveyance to a life imagined only in my dreams.

Turning on my heel I had studied the tumbled ruins of a fort built by the Dutch in the seventeenth century to defend this tiny island possession against the depredations of marauding buccaneers and the ever-invading land hungry British. The fort was now just a tumbled mound of giant granite blocks, however in my imagination, I had visualised Dutch gunners at their cannons, defying the tall sailing ships bringing these terrible invaders from the sea. Time and space and place stood still etched forever on my inner being. No going back this was why I had chosen to be a seaman with the world at my feet.

We had sailed soon after this epiphany and *Barranca* had headed almost due east, threading a course through the scattered islands just off the north coast of South America. Steaming between Granada and Trinidad Tobago into the Guiana Basin, and then altering course she headed south passing on her starboard side the borders of Venezuela and French Guiana, and keeping the continent well to starboard veered easterly to keep the shallows around the dreaded and infamous Devils Island well away from her keel. Butting into the choppy swell raised by the Equatorial counter current, we steered due east again and then south, crossing the Equator to weather the penal island of Fernando de Naronha, then south by west to the port of Recife perched on the north easterly tip of the state of Pernambuco.

Rousing from my reverie with a painful moan, I climbed stiffly from the bunk and returned to the present. I grimaced at my battered nose and black eyes in the cabin mirror and returned to the pantry amongst the laughter and catcalls of my shipmates in the galley.

· · · · ·

By daybreak that morning the stevedore had his dockers aboard and the bosun had the covers off the forward hatch. Such is the limited capacity of this port that no cranes exist to aid discharge of cargo. The deck crew rigged the ship's lifting gear which is supported by Samson posts, huge steel stanchions bolted to the steel deck, powered by steam driven winches the drums of which run steel cables through blocks and pulleys. The noise is almost deafening, and the pain in my nose and a thumping head did not help my humour.

I attended to my chores amongst the hustle and bustle, clang and bang, of cargo being lifted from the hold. The air within the accommodation became stifling. With the engine stopped, no air circulated through the 'punkah louvres', a primitive ventilation system, and not a single breeze offered relief. Stores for the galley arrived at 1500 hours and the entire catering staff had to forego their after lunch rest period and get them aboard. Heavy sweaty work this, creating a surprising shortness of temper, the usual banter and jolly smiles noticeably absent as was old Monty, lazy bastard should have paid off years ago. The chief cook stayed below in the cool-room, (the refrigeration driven by on board generators), supervising the stowing and the second stood on the wharf checking off invoices. The rest of us staggered up and down the gangway under heavy sides of beef and lamb, sacks of flour, and many cases of tinned goods.

Suddenly there came a huge bellow from the cool-room, followed by a clatter of feet as Winston flew up the companionway and streaked through the galley with Ambrose hot on his heels. 'Stop him! Stop the crazy bastard,' yelled the panicking Winston.

Pausing only long enough to select a large knife from a rack in the galley Ambrose chased the chief along the forward deck. He baled Winston up against the hatch coaming, the knife flashed and blood poured from a slash in the forearm of our chubby chief cook. All hell broke out as crewmembers scattered in all directions, only Angus the bosun kept his cool. Walking forward purposefully with his hand held out almost in supplication, his brown eyes flat, devoid of emotion, he asked in a quiet voice, 'Give me the blade man.'

A tense silence enveloped the deck and nobody moved. The sun scorched off the steel deck plates. The eyes in Ambrose's head were wild, the skin on his face yellow and drum tight, the high cheekbones carved with tension. The moment was palpable. Winston's eyes rolled in his now grey face then he pissed in his pants the ammonia smell heavy in the electric air. Mouth agape I stood stock still, a carton of tinned milk balanced on my shoulder. The scene, tableau-like, until the steel ladder from the bridge to the deck echoed to running feet as the Captain and first officer scrambled down from their eyrie on the bridge breaking the tension. The mate held a large six shot service revolver secured by a lanyard around his neck. The fire went out of Ambrose, the flashing green eyes died to ashes, his shoulders slumped in resignation and he handed the knife handle first to Angus. They marched the unprotesting Ambrose aft to the hospital where they secured him to the metal tubing of the bunks. An ambulance whisked Winston away to shore side emergency and everyone settled down again.

The Chief Steward, pale after the incident, was all a dither because there was not a single person left to cook the evening meal. He explained that somehow Ambrose had obtained a bottle of rum and under its influence an old grudge between the two men had blossomed.

'I'd like to catch the bastard who brought the grog aboard. Hey you two', he yelled pointing to Chester and me, 'grab hold of some of that fresh bread we just took on board and make up a heap of sandwiches, while I boil a great pot of soup, that's all they'll be getting tonight!' Charlie the 2nd steward took the stores from below and lent a hand.

By this time both of us had overcome the shock of our favourite cook, a normally placid man flying off the handle in such frenzy. Shaken by this new experience in our young lives we complied in an almost spiritual silence. For myself, this coming hard on the heels of Recife, began as a tangle of emotions, a strangely painful thought process began unravelling slowly in my skull. Was it to be always like this? This kind violence was new to me, at school there had been bullies to fight. I had represented my school in the boxing ring so they rarely came near me. Street gangs not unusual in London's suburbs were usually found in dance halls and youth clubs; however this was on a whole new level. I was no coward and as a rule could give as well as I got. Knives, bottles and chairs were a whole new ball game. I treasured the freedom of the open sea and sky, the mystery of foreign shores, now I wondered at the cost. There was no escape; this voyage would last several more months. Determined to see it through with as little trouble as possible, I quietly turned to my cabin mate Chester he looked grey, the smile gone from his chubby face and then he turned to the second, 'What was the gun for Charlie he weren't going to shoot him was he?'

'That my son was in case of panic, you would be surprised at the folly and frailty of us humans in the face of violence. All that macho stuff is strictly for Hollywood. The show of discipline from on high usually calms everyone down, now get on with it.' He had said a mouthful.

While we busied ourselves with a mountain of sandwiches, the local police arrived aboard wanting to cart Ambrose off to the jail house. However the skipper would not allow it until the British Consul arrived. This in fact never happened, as there was no such person in Recife at that time. An hour went by and eventually the gendarmes left smelling suspiciously of the captain's best malt whiskey. Word went round that they would sail on time as per schedule the next day.

Later that evening I took Ambrose a mug of soup and a cheese sandwich. The weird green eyes glared up at me, his clothes smelled of sweat and an odour not unlike vinegar spread through the small cabin. The cold glare he gave me sent a shiver down my spine.

'Steady on mate, I'm on your side, what brought that lot on then?

'That bastard's been riding me all trip,' Ambrose snarled, 'back home I dated his sister a couple of times and he didn't like it plus I'm a better cook than that bastard will ever be.'

I could not fathom this, why would one Negro denigrate another because he had darker skin? Granted the fat roly poly chief was of an ebony hue. Puzzling over this I later enquired of Chester.

'Oh it's common enough', explained Chester 'we are often harder on each other in a social sense than you whites, and it's all a matter of pulling the girls. For some reason they prefer the lighter skinned mulattos. I dunno why skin colour is so important. Personally I haven't got a hope.' He gave me a rueful smile full of solemn thoughts. 'You'll do alright,' I said with a grin, 'especially with your sense of humour.'

The knife, the heat, the rum, and the jealousy all seemed too strong a mixture to be believed. My thoughts ran up hill and down dale. Winston with a heavily bandaged arm returned in the early hours of the morning.

· · · · ·

We now commenced to voyage south calling at several small ports, staying sometimes only a few hours, all the while discharging our goods, until we arrived in Puerto Alegre.

The slow trip south had taken several days, during which time the bruising and the black eyes caused by the flying ashtray had faded. I had learned a painful but valuable lesson. On arrival Ambrose was hustled from the hospital and whisked away by an official from the British High Commission with a police escort and no more heard from him. Meanwhile Winston, nursing his injured arm as much as possible, once again controlled the galley with Chester working overtime to make up for the loss of Ambrose.

At Porto Alegre the air was much cooler and a prevailing south easterly helped to keep the cabins from the swelter of the northerly climes. The town itself appeared to be much more substantial. Wide paved boulevards connected tree lined squares which contained ornamental fountains. Buildings of an obvious Iberian influence constructed mainly of local stone also displayed facades of what could only be blue granite brought out as ballast in Portuguese ships of a bygone age. Modern, stylish cafés and restaurants sat beneath deep shadowed verandas and cool arcades of shops ran back from the verandas.

However all of this was still to be discovered as I toiled away at the routine of shipboard life. This dockside had cranes so rigging the ship's hoists was not necessary, and the loading went on at a steady quieter pace. Forklift trucks buzzed busily from long low sheds and dockers of every shade of brown in tattered shorts and t-shirts, no hard hats or safety boots, placed boxes and canisters into huge rope slings to be carried aboard and lowered into the waiting maw of our holds. Amidst all this under a favourable sky the skipper had all the deck hands painting the ship's sides with red lead to try and stem the advancing rust. On the concrete wharf crewmen with long rollers dodged among the hustle and bustle painting furiously and somehow got the job done. Whilst on the seaward side men hung in cradles that are raised and lowered by ropes as each section is completed.

I now had extra duties. Chester, to his delight, had been promoted to assistant cook, and many of his old chores fell on my shoulders.

The boss of the shore side stevedores now sat at lunch in the officer's saloon, obviously a perk of the job; he was a small neat man with a carefully combed head of jet black hair always dressed in an immaculate white short sleeved shirt with a plain grey necktie. Peering through the servery hatch I noticed that his darkly intelligent eyes missed nothing.

One afternoon a couple of days into the loading, I sat chatting with the bosun way down aft, sheltered from a chilly southerly by the poop overhang. Seated on steel bollards and gazing about at all the activity we did not notice the quiet approach of the stevedore.

'May I join you?' Not waiting for a reply he looked at me and continued, 'I have noticed what a busy lad you are,' this stated in accented but good English.

'We are short handed,' I replied. Angus rose politely and muttering something about going back to work, headed off down the port side. Taking a leather case from his pocket, the stranger offered me a cigar. At my refusal, he selected one for himself and sat on the empty bollard.

'My name is Edourdo and you are Tom, the chief told me.' We fell easily into conversation.

'Tell me Tom all you English people sound different when you speak, and yet it is all the same language. We have uneducated natives from the interior who are peasants who murder our Portuguese language, they rarely mingle or talk to us city folk. Unless they speak in a patois Portuguese we don't communicate. However there is a difference in pronunciation and tone with your people, and it takes a little concentration to understand what is said to me by all British peoples, how is that?'

'Firstly we are not all Englishmen; our little group of islands is inhabited by descendants of many races. Although originally European tribes mainly Celts, crossed over from France in the Ice Age, our forefathers also suffered subsequent invasions from Romans, Normans and Vikings, pushing the Celtic peoples into the Northern and Western parts of the main island. These hilly, craggy regions have the modern names of Scotland in the north, and Wales in the west. They have a common language called Gaelic. Smaller islands off the shores of Scotland, because of their isolation, use this Celtic tongue an ancient and poetic language but speak English on the mainland. The largest of the islands to the west of Wales across a narrow strip of sea is called Ireland, and here the Celtic tribes have survived and multiplied. Despite England's depredations over the centuries these tough independent people have maintained their individuality which is reflected in their speech. Therefore a Scot, a Welshman and an Irishman will have a turn of phrase and an intonation totally different to an Englishman and to add to the confusion the English spoken in the North Country will sound different to that of a person from the south. This is also true in Scotland

and Ireland.' I stopped self consciously, what was I doing lecturing this fellow? 'What about you, where are you from?' I explained that I was born and raised on the border of south London and the county of Surrey.

'Our local way of speech for the average person is fairly bland, with an overlay of Cockney, which you might call a patois if pushed. It stems from the proximity of our capital city. Educated people tend to pronounce words very carefully.'

'My goodness', the stevedore exclaimed again 'what a smart fellow you are'.

'Not really', I said, 'we learn all this stuff in junior school, it's there if you are interested enough, and I read a lot at sea.'

'Olla!' the stevedore exclaimed 'you interest me greatly, come, you must meet my family, and take dinner with us while I tell you about Brazil'.

'Blimey mate, I'm working tonight, and I eat my dinner standing up at the pantry bench'.

'Barbaric', cried the little man tiny hands beating the air, 'come I will fetch you at eight o clock, I'll fix it with the Chief Steward'. Astonished at this generosity I stammered my thanks and asked, 'what do I wear sir?'

'Just a shirt and slacks will do fine', was the easy reply.

At eight on the dot an old blue Buick Sedan eased to a halt at the gangway and Eduardo half opened the door and leaning out waved me down the gangway. The smiling ladies of the family were all seated in the rear of the spacious car. I was introduced to Mama Imelda, eldest daughter Evita and the younger girl Elena. They were a handsome group with pearly white teeth contrasting with a dusky complexion and long tresses of raven black hair.

A short drive took us to a pleasant square surrounded by colonnaded footpaths upon which half the population seemed to be strolling. Parking easily as there seemed to be little traffic about, we stepped out into the cool of the evening. Mother Imelda stood several inches taller than her husband with a full figure, whilst the girls were petite like their father. The younger Elena chattered away in Portuguese a constant barrage that of course went over my head. Eduardo tried to translate with apologies for her manners, but Evita a girl of around my own age walked silently beside her father.

'This is what we call in our language the evening passado,' explained Eduardo 'we walk here among our friends and neighbours gossiping about this and that before retiring to our evening meal at around nine or ten o clock. Once a week we eat here on the square'.

In addition, the boys check out the girls I thought with a smile at Evita whose eyes had been roaming all around. At a small sidewalk café, the family were greeted with a great flapping of napkins by the staff; they smiled all around at the other diners who waved cordially. With a courteous bow a waiter placed a jug containing fresh limes and mint with ice cubes and water upon the table. In the square people wandered arm in arm, soft music wafted on a gentle breeze.

'Tom you must try this drink it is very refreshing, however, you may have beer if you prefer.'

'No sir this is fine'.

During the meal, a delicious fish dish with onions tomatoes and peppers, I wondered why I had been chosen for this warm and generous invitation. Conversation became one sided as the ladies had not a word of English. The air in the square carried delicious aromas of food and coffee, and the scent of flowers on the zephyr of a breeze. Across the square in the ornate entrance to a stately hotel I saw a pair of guitarists wandering amongst the patrons the gentle serenades carried softly on the air.

The meal concluded we all piled into the Buick and I was whisked back to the *Barranca*. With smiling goodbyes all round and with a wave and a 'Bon voyage', they were gone. My head still buzzed with the why of it all. A full moon floated in silver glory as I mounted the gangway still dazed by my good fortune. Three officers stood leaning on the rail smoking in companionable silence as I climbed aboard.

'Aha my lad' greeted the Chief Steward, 'how was it?'

'Fantastic thanks Mr Cassidy, but I'm puzzled .Why me?'

'Well son, I decided after your nasty experience in Recife, and that nasty business with the cooks, a good run ashore with respectable people would set your head right.'

'Thanks chief you bet it did they are wonderful folks'. Resolving to remain in touch with these generous Brazilians I went sleepily to my bunk. Chester snored quietly in the adjacent bunk. The porthole and stormwater scuttle were raised on a hook to catch any passing breeze. Suddenly a drunken face appeared at the port. It was Monty, mumbling in a strange incoherent manner, his intoxicated tongue slithered over his prominent yellow teeth and mouthing weird imprecations. He attempted to climb through the small aperture but fell back with a clatter to the deck. Both of us awoke in fright.

'Get the hell away from there you idiot,' I yelled. Chester, very angry to be awakened, quickly locked the cabin door. Monty's contorted face had reappeared. I approached the porthole somewhat afraid, 'If you don't get away I'll drop this scuttle on your fingers you maniac'. Chester threw a glass of water in the grotesque features.

Having come into contact with homosexuals in our short lives at sea, both of us now became suspicious of the so immaculate and obliging Monty. The next morning he hung his head and apologised, I never trusted his friendly advances again. Before going to sea training school I had worked as a trainee waiter it two smart central London hotels. Several of the waiters were lonely ex-patriot Europeans displaced at the end of World War II. I mistook their friendly overtures as being the normal actions of lonely men in a strange city. I woke up to that damn quick smart when baled up with a proposition by one of the night porters. I also encountered much of the same in training school and on my first voyage. I found it best to say friendly thanks, but no thanks to save unpleasantness.

· · ···

Montevideo came next. Monte as everyone aboard calls this harbour city, is famous for a notable British victory at sea in the mouth of the River Platte during World War II. The fast German cruiser *Graf Spey*, was caught by three British ships, which blockaded her exit from this neutral port, and after a fierce engagement accepted her captain's gallant surrender.

Shore leave is denied all hands, and *Barranca* is in and away in a matter of hours.

Now we head northward, back on our tracks, homeward bound. A displaced British seaman joined us in Monte as second cook. Chester was back to standard galley boy and me, thank God, back to normal duties.

Santos the port for Sao Paulo is the next landfall. Santos is a typical seaport with cranes and sheds and busy dockers. Across the basin the tall buildings of a large city beckon as if to say come and explore Brazil's second city, for only Rio de Janeiro has more to offer.

Later that evening, with the chief's permission, I answered that call and summoning a taxi, dressed in my best suit, I took the fifteen-minute drive to Sao Paulo. In my wallet I carried five pounds sterling. Asking the driver to drop me at a Bureau de Change, I cashed the lot and found that I had more than one thousand Cruzeiros. I was amazed at the size of the denominations of the colourful currency, hundreds, two hundreds and even a five hundred note and some change. Peeling off a fifty, I handed it to the driver who gave me thirty in change. The value of an English pound suddenly hit like a physical blow and hurrying back inside the Bureau I put all the big notes into the back of a leather wallet I carried and the remainder in my trouser pocket. Shipboard stories of sailors being robbed rang through my brain.

Remembering that late evening is the time that the locals took the air, I strolled forth and quickly realised I stood out, a foreigner in a heavy blue suit. Quickly removing my jacket and hanging it over my shoulder by the loop and loosening my tie I preceded as nonchalantly as possible. The citizens of Sao Paulo all looked very cool in lightweight clothes, the men in open neck shirts. Feeling very overdressed I knew I stood out like a cockroach at a picnic. Once again I wandered through arcades and piazzas, cafes and restaurants that filled the evening air with tempting aromas. I seated myself at an empty table beneath an awning with a view of children paddling in a nearby fountain I ordered what the menu stated was a beefy steak and a cold beer. The meal that arrived comprised a fillet mignon with all the trimmings and the Brahma Chop lager filled the glass with icy bubbles, to my astonishment it only cost the equivalent of about five shillings in British money. Once again feeling the weight of the money in my wallet I resolved to head straight back to the ship. Hailing a passing taxi I sat back marvelling at the way of life a warm and sunny land could bestow on its inhabitants. London's grey, narrow, gritty and bustling streets filled with traffic and scurrying crowds seemed a lifetime away.

On impulse deciding on another beer, I stopped the cab a short distance from the entrance to the dock gates. On the perimeter of my vision across the ancient cobble stones a cantina shed an inviting glow from lanterns hung on an outside gallery. I entered, it seemed quiet by dockside standards and no other member of the crew was present. No more than half a dozen patrons sat at the bar and tables all of which were clean and gentle Latin rhythms added a soothing atmosphere. A short balding barman with a shiny dome with close set sparkling hazel eyes on either side of a huge broken nose and a clean apron asked my pleasure. As usual I ordered a local beer and sat back thinking about my evening with a contented smile.

'Ello Ingles,' a soft voice whispered in my ear. Startled, turning I saw a rather pretty girl of about my own age at my elbow. Her approach had been so quiet that I could not resist a glance at her feet which clad in ballerina style slippers, much like those worn by fashion conscious girls back home, showed a pretty ankle beneath a modest calf length skirt.

'Buy me a drink Johnny?'

'Sure what will you have?'

'An orange juice thanks you.' Her accent intrigued me and correcting her on my name, we chatted for a while until she whispered,

'You want come with me for a good time Tommy?'

Many nocturnal fumblings with girls back home plus the talk of the lads aboard ship had given me a good clue as to what this 'good time' was all about. Back home I'd had a girlfriend since the age of fourteen. Gentle Maureen with her big cow eyes and demure manner, we had been real childhood sweethearts. We had met at the local youth club and had 'smooched' to the crooners like Perry Como and Eddie Fisher, and jived to the big swing bands and lately rocked to Bill Haley. We kissed until our lips were sore on her parents door step; I fumbled on auto pilot for her breasts until the shrill call of her mother ordered her inside. Strangely, I thought of her at this moment, it must have been the shoes. 'What's your name?' I asked.

'Marina', she replied.

'OK, so how much do you charge, quanta costa?' I asked, showing off my smattering of Portuguese and rubbing my fingers together in the international sign of how much.

31

'One hundred Cruzeiros' the softly spoken reply, a gentle smile lit Marina's face and a kind of mischief flickered in her soft brown eyes, she knew a virgin when she saw one. Well, I thought now is as good a time as any; she looked young and fresh and safe and ten bob is OK.

Taking me by the hand Marina walked us around a nearby corner and into a small hotel. Inside only blue light globes illuminated the interior; I became apprehensive of the surroundings hesitating in the small vestibule. The concierge waved a cheerful hello.

Marina took me over to the desk, 'fifty Cruzeiros for the room', she giggled in my ear.

'S*** what comes next,' I muttered forking out the dough. The room, stark white, but bathed in the same pale blue glow had one large bed plumb centre, only one purpose here. In one graceful shrug Marina stood naked before me. Oh well in for a penny and in for a pound, off came the gear and I jumped straight onto the bed. No shyness now, with senses swimming with delight I found soft velvet curves, lithe tangled limbs; a pungent earthy smell clung to her willing body. Our healthy young limbs searched again and again for climactic release, then deep peaceful sleep. I fell asleep with muscles turned to jelly and a warm lassitude tinged with a little guilt that I had not saved this moment for Maureen, her face floated like a chimera in my dream that night.

Awaking before dawn I swung my feet to the floor with quick alarm. The bed was empty, I naturally panicked. Leaping to my pile of clothes, I checked all the pockets, heart racing seconds passed as I fumbled for the wallet which much to my surprise was in tact. Heaving a thankful sigh I dressed and descended to the foyer. The same smiling guardian stood on watch and with a weary wave and a smile he bade me 'Adios.'

Later that morning back on duty Chester, who had noticed the hour of my return, wanted to know the whole story. Still a little bemused by the night's events I only shook my head before replying, 'Mate do you realise that in this beautiful country a man can get a great meal, a few beers, and a night with a lovely lady for a little over a quid?'

'Show me where!' yelled Chester.

'Sorry mate, no more shore leave for me in this port, let's wait until we get to Rio'.

Presently the radio officer/ship's doctor bustled into our cabin and raced me off to the hospital. 'Listen son', he began, 'in this part of the world you have to take precautions know what I mean?'

'No,' was my innocent response.

'The officer on gangway watch told me you did not come aboard until 0500 that can only mean one thing. Well Romeo, among the local tarts V.D. is rife and I don't suppose you took precautions so take hold of this and do yourself a favour'.

Passing me a small packet with a tube within the officer bustled out again without another word. The reality struck home with a thud upon reading the instructions. I applied the substance with a grimace of distaste. Surely not Marina, but then she was a whore. All the romance dissipated with a sadness which I found hard to explain to myself. I realised in one sense that sex was great; however the manner of the liaison was critical to the afterglow. Resuming my work, I once again mused on the voyage so far. First the glory of the Caribbean and tropic nights, then the drama with Ambrose, the sights, the smells, the ecstasy of Santos, a jumble and tumble of thoughts and ideas skim helter skelter through my brain. Conclusion, I was definitely enjoying myself although the blood and snot of fist fights would never appeal as a regular escape valve which is the memory locker in which I placed the previous dramas.

Later that morning, seated on the after deck, sipping coffee with the bosun, who had become something of a father figure, I related my experience. 'It's called growing up son. You're a good lad, a bit soft perhaps, but that'll change.' I decided to confide in Angus about my guilty feelings in regard to Maureen.

'Angus' I said, 'I never had a dad to talk to me about life and such, and being brought up in a house full of females, I find life is getting a bit heavy, you know, sudden like, confusing. I have a girl back home and we never did the business,' guilty pause, 'you know?'

I hung my head a little ashamed of my confession. A man of very few words Angus shrugged his broad shoulders. 'You're doing alright son, as I said a bit soft , but I've seen a lot worse. You'll do in the long run; just take it easy with hookers.'

Rising from our usual seat, he gave me a slap on the back, and with a nod and a wink, walked forward yelling orders to the toiling deck hands.

Returning to my chores a few minutes later along the steel deck I came upon Robbie McGregor an ordinary seaman chipping away at layers of old paint. Despite his Scottish sounding name Rob is a Cockney from the East End of London. Tall, with long dark curly hair and a deep sun tan Macgregor stopped banging away at the stubborn deck paint and speaking from his crouched position said with a grin,

'They tell me you are a bit of a lad with the girls matey.'

Before this only a casual nod had passed between us. I gave him a nod with what I hoped was a worldly air. This tall young seaman at least five years my senior and hardened by years of hard work on deck in all weathers grinned mischievously.

'You need looking after you do, when we get to Rio me and the Guinea will take you under our wings. The "Sheilas" there will knock your socks off.' Mac had sailed to Australia a couple of times.

Not sure how to take this offer I grinned again, the Guinea referred to is another seaman roughly McGregor's age and known as a hard case.

Just at that moment a loud nasal Liverpool accented voice yelled,

'Hey, you Morgan get your butt in here and get some work done!'

'See you later Rob', I muttered and fled into the pantry where the chief's red face continued to glare. 'You are getting too big for your boots lad,' he roared, and storming off down the alleyway, he nearly collided with Winston and Chester eavesdropping from the galley door with huge white toothy grins splitting their ebony faces.

• • • • •

The view of Rio from the sea is breathtaking. The pilot brought *Barranca* gently steaming through calm cobalt waters under a cloudless sky. To our left, on the port side, the Sugarloaf Mountain soared heavenward as if to lift the giant figure of Christ closer to the ethereal paradise. Immediately forward, straight off the bow the city proper raised tall buildings as a backdrop to the teeming beaches. On the starboard side hills rose up in a parade of green until finally fading into a haze of misty purple.

The docks, a straggle of cranes and sheds, seemed to be a part of the city centre and the pilot took *Barranca* in a lazy curve to our berth on this bright Saturday morning, without the assistance of tugs. The month of May in these latitudes provides long sunlit days. From the berth I could see the people moving in the streets native Brasileiros of every hue, from golden brown to a dark milk chocolate and a black that was almost purple.

All meals over for the day and the pantry cleaned and scrubbed down, I took the night watch keeper's supper up to the bridge. As I placed the tray on the bench behind the chart house the skipper appeared.

'Ah! Morgan you'll be going ashore tonight?'

'Yes sir, with a couple of senior hands.'

'Very well young fella, no repeats of Recife, is that clearly understood?'

'Yes sir,' I replied with a courteous touch of my forehead, 'you can count on it.'

Accompanied by McGregor and the deckhand known as Guinea, dressed as usual in faded blue jeans and t-shirts, I wandered ashore around 1800 hours. The night had begun to close in, the warm balmy sapphire air intoxicating. Beyond the dock gates the colourful throng of people seemed to dance along in a kind of shuffle that started at the hips. I had the feeling that a sort of Saturday night release permeated the atmosphere. The handsome smiling men, women, and children, all moved to an inner tempo that was infectious. The citizens of Rio are known as Cariocas, and they were off to make the most of the weekend. I remembered a Disney character; a dancing parrot, from my childhood called Jose Carioca, and now understood the association. A cashmere breeze wafted inviting aromas and cooled my face.

As we strolled we came upon a street market; a litter of stalls surrounded by hundreds of people. We pushed our way through the jostling throng. Vendors shouted their wares in a raucous chorus. Fruit and vegetables of every hue and shape lay colourfully displayed, birds in cages and parrots on stands, even tiny monkeys on light chains joined in the din. On a stall full of interesting local carvings, a serving tray for tea or drinks caught my marvelling eye. Roughly two feet by one and a half feet, the tray made from polished inlaid hardwoods, had shimmering blue butterfly wings under glass as a decoration, a truly lovely piece of workmanship. I asked the price.

'Ten dollars U.S.' replied the toothless grinning vendor his face as wrinkled as a prune.

'Bulls*** Tom,' this from Guinea, 'I'll bet you can get it for a quid, two hundred Cruzeiros. Tell 'him we're not Yanks.'

'My mum would go a bundle on that,' I said.

'Come back tomorrow mate and offer him a quid for it.'

Easing our way onward through the crowd we came upon a broad main street. Huge strange multi coloured paving slabs made up the wide sidewalks, soft yellows, and faded pinks, lay amidst the standard cement grey. Slender trees dotted a uniform distance apart graced the handsome boulevard. Clanging tramcars ferried passengers, some hanging from the sides and American made automobiles cruised by with occupants that hung their arms from open windows smiling huge white smiles. A silver moon lit the scene. The air smelled of rotting fruit, coffee, petrol guzzling autos, and sea salt.

We walked on for about a half mile, and reached an intersection where another similar street crossed, and came upon a sight that caused us to stop in our tracks.

Parked at the centre of the junction a huge army tank commanded the intersection, the long muzzle of the turret gun pointing straight at us. Four or five soldiers with rifles slung on their backs lounged nearby dressed in battle fatigues, they glowered at the passing parade of citizens most of whom totally ignored them.

'You'd better behave tonight Guinea or you'll have those ugly bastards on your case.' Mac exclaimed,

'That couldn't be worse than the bosun's boot continually poised adjacent to my butt,' quipped Guinea.

Very soon as we strolled along marvelling at all we saw, a wide curving promenade arcing south took us to the fabled Copacabana beach. Cafés, bars and 1940's style high-rise buildings jostled for space. Seemingly lying in wait for us, a huge pink neon sign announced in the gathering dusk, 'THE FLAMINGO'.

'Right, come on lads time for a beer,' a grinning Guinea declared with an enthusiastic rub of calloused hands.

Inside the bar we realised that this place is a very up market restaurant and cabaret. The furnishings very chic, stainless steel with polished gleaming surfaces, were scattered invitingly. Not the average joint that seamen would frequent. The beers came in tall frosted pilsner glasses and cost about one U.S. dollar each.

Carrying the glasses to an outside table we watched the gentle curve of lapping surf. Sand dimpled by many footsteps, crumbling sand castles, and shallow hollowed out pools, stood as testament to the sunny day, as families, who with umbrellas folded, gathered up chattering infants and melted into the darkening night.

'Too bad,' said Mac sadly, 'we've missed all the bikini clad babes, what say we try for an afternoon off tomorrow, as it's Sunday we could come back for a swim. 'Good idea son,' agreed Guinea, 'what are your chances Morg?'

'Not good mate that Scouse git is on my back over Recife and Santos.'

Tom studied Guinea's sun bronzed face and asked,

"Why do people call you Guinea, what's your real name?"

The grey sleepy appearing eyes took on a wary glint, as if he was about to ask what it had to do with me. Then he smiled a whimsical softening of the hard features. 'My dad was a street trader, you know barrow boys we call 'em now, he pushed a cart around the streets of Whitechapel all his life. I came along a bit late in the scene, and as the baby with golden hair, he named me George, same as the old king. With hair as bright as a newly minted guinea coin, the old boy decided I was lucky, and would rub my head every morning as he left saying, 'bring us luck today Guinea,' it stuck and I prefer it to George so there you go.'

I studied the young seaman's weather-beaten features and decided that time, wind, sun and storms on deck had dulled the golden boy's image. Mac left to get more beer and Guinea leaning close said in a confidential tone,

'Now listen Morg, you've got a lot to learn my son, first you never pay the asking price in these market places, perhaps in a joint like this you have no choice, but elsewhere you have to haggle this ain't Marks and Spencers. The locals will take you for a mug if you don't, they expect it and enjoy it O.K.? Another thing if you are with us next trip, stock up with Pac-a-Macs and reels of cotton from Woolworths, your mate in Puerto Alegre will take all you can supply at three times the price you paid for it, good beer money sunshine.' Nylon Pac-a-Macs designed to fit into a pocket were ideal for a country with a climate that was afflicted by sudden unforeseeable drenching showers of rain. I guessed Guinea had learned a lot from his old man.

The terrace began to fill up with the pre-dinner crowd and we decided to call it a day and head back. On our arrival completely sober and early the watch aboard could hardly believe their eyes. Mac gave me a conspiratorial wink, 'This should impress your boss; see how you go for a half day off tomorrow.'

Sundays on board a ship in port are slow and easy. With no cargo discharging all is quiet, and most of the officers are ashore doing what officers do, presumably. Much to my surprise, Hopalong gave me the rest of the day after lunch to myself. Rushing down to the seaman's accommodation I cried, 'c'mon you blokes let's get to it.'

Fifteen minutes later, swimming trunks wrapped in towels tucked under our arms, we set off like schoolboys on a spree. Grabbing a taxi we were on the beach in twenty minutes and in the gently breaking surf in two. Copacabana Beach on a Sunday in mid November is bedlam with families, screaming kids, posing bikini-clad girls, idiots playing soccer, plus a beach ball game or three. Standing shoulder deep in the warm lapping waves Mac looking to the mayhem on the beach said, 'I feel a lot safer out here, can you see where we left our towels?'

'Don't worry mate, with *S.S. Barranca* written all over 'em no one will take 'em,' predicted Guinea more in hope than conviction.

On emerging from the sea we soon located the towels and sprawled on the sand. Three tanned strapping young fellows do not go unnoticed on many beaches, however here on this beach we were just one of the crowds. Mac's gaze wandered up to the terrace of the Flamingo. Gaily coloured umbrellas fluttered in the cooling sea breeze. 'Look you blokes there are birds up there at the café, let's go take a look see.'

'Trust you Mac, what's wrong with the water?'

'It's all right for you Morg, you got your end away in Santos, Mac and me are staving for our oats.'

'Nah, you blokes go ahead, I'm staying here for a while yet.'

'There'll be nothing left by the time you get there pal.'

'You two go on I'll be fine down here.'

Scooping up their gear the two desperados headed for the changing shack, and then up the beach, across the promenade and into the bar. Meanwhile I swam lazily just outside the breaking waves and the main crowd of bathers for another ten minutes or so and then headed in. Once seated on my tiny towel, I looked casually around. Two teenage girls looked across and giggled, I rolled onto my stomach and dozed off.

Awakening a few minutes later, I immediately looked up at the café. No sign of Guinea or Mac. Quickly showering in the changing shed and pulling on my faded jeans and a checked sport shirt, and dodging the Sunday traffic made a bee line for the café. My dark brown hair sun bleached on the ends had by this time grown long, and it was still dripping wet when I strode into the Flamingo. Enquiring at the bar about the two Englishmen, the barman gave me a knowing wink and said with a smile,

'They will not be long senor, have a beer while you wait.' I paused to take stock of the place, it seemed that everyone was on the terrace, chatting, laughing, and sipping at long cool drinks, very relaxed. 'Ok pal, make it a rum and coke.'

She was blonde with blue eyes, and a cheeky smile. My first reaction was how unusual her colouring was in a Latin country. The slim waist encased in tailored figure hugging slacks looked promising. Ordering a banana Daiquiri she parked on the stool next to me, there were several empty stools on either side. While the barman filled her order I glanced casually around the bar, she seemed to be alone.

'Can I get that for you?' I asked hopefully in a quiet voice.

She turned amazingly blue eyes upon me, a tiny smile lurking in their depths.

'My name is Miranda,' was all she said, brushing a stray strand of hair from her cheek.

'Well hello,' I said holding out my hand, 'I'm Tom.'

'So you are Ingles, I thought you might have been American.'

'Sorry to disappoint you, just a poor seaman on a day ashore. Tell me how come you speak good English?'

'Not all our people have the opportunity to learn, many of them in the poorer districts have no, how do you say, conception, but us working girls meet many tourists.'

Working girls! Oh no not again, or was I being naive. That teasing, cheeky smile hovered in her lovely eyes. I fell into their blue pools. 'So Miranda, what do you do?' I asked tongue in cheek.

'I'm an air hostess with Varig Airlines the Brazilian offshoot of Pan American' came the reply with a merry twinkle, 'you thought I was a hooker didn't you?'

I sat in stunned silence, what can a guy say.

'Look Tom the truth is I have a forty eight hour stopover in Rio. My home is in Santos. Early Tuesday we fly to Jamaica, and then Florida. You look lonely and I've no friends here, what say we have dinner together?'

Miranda's English was excellent if tinged with a little Deep South North American drawl which I found fascinating. 'Miranda' I stammered, 'I'd love to, I don't want to sound like a bum, but I have limited cash.'

'Sure, that's fine however not here it's far too expensive, let's try around the corner away from the bright lights and we can split the bill O.K.? I nervously agreed; was I being suckered into something here?

'O.K., but let's not stray far away from the main streets.' Perhaps the tanks and soldiers might provide protection if I needed it. I couldn't resist the question, 'by the way what's the story on the troops everywhere?'

'Oh, El Presidente and his gang of crooks are fleecing the poor as usual, and in the country the peasants are really pissed off, unrest everywhere. You know the old story of how the rich get rich on the backs of the poor.' Taking my arm she said, 'That's enough of that, come let us enjoy. Tell me about yourself.'

Thereafter, the most pleasant evening of my young life began. If Miranda noticed the age gap between us it never showed in her manner, which was witty and warmly interested in my life.

We found a cosy, inexpensive cantina and settling into a comfy booth dined early by Brazilian standards. Around nine o'clock I began to think it was time to say goodnight and head back to the ship. But a voice in the back of my head kept repeating, 'try your luck, you never know, she may be waiting for you to make the first move.' The Portuguese wine and spicy food, the soft music by candlelight was intoxicating, soon we became very mellow and content in one another's company.

'You know Miranda; I have to start work at five a.m. tomorrow. I'd better get back to my ship,' Leaning across the table to give her a friendly thank you kiss on the cheek she turned full face and kissed me on the lips.

'Tommy it is far too early to call it a night, come, you are in Rio on a beautiful Sunday night. Cariocas do not sleep until the early hours; I want to show you something.'

'Ah', here it comes thought yours truly, because an element of doubt about her motives still clouded my perception. Miranda hugged my arm tight to her side; I could feel the soft swell of her breast as she led me through narrow streets of deep blue shadows to a small hotel. The warm night air carried murmurings and muted music from behind shuttered windows. My nerve ends tingled with nervous energy. Still doubting her intentions, I was ushered into a small foyer filled with heavy European style furniture polished to a high degree. Behind an ornate desk a solidly built man with crew cut grey hair and rimless eyeglasses greeted Miranda in what sounded to me to be German.

'Greetings my leibchen'

'Good evening Uncle Franz. May we have coffee and schnapps please?'

'But of course, come, come, sit, sit,' he bustled from behind the desk calling over his shoulder to his wife,

'Carlotta come quickly; bring coffee for Miranda and her friend.'

Franz ducked under the ornate staircase located immediately behind the desk and popped up like a rabbit from a hat behind a tiny bar. Facing us to the left of the bar a small lounge full of heavy leather armchairs looked cosy, lacy antimacassar covered the backs and arms, an aroma of Potpourri blended nicely with the 1930's ambience. He poured three measures of clear liquid into three chilled glasses

'So, tell me leibchen, who is your friend?'

'This is Tommy, he is English, and Franz no war talk, promise me, he is too young to know anything about it.' Remembering the Blitz only too well I shrugged and held out my hand to shake with the old guy. Later Mirada explained her parents were German migrants and Franz her father's brother. 'We do not have the English here very often, mostly American, welcome mien Herr', he called from his position behind the tiny bar.

The hotelkeeper's wife bustled in with a tray of minute cups and a pot of steaming coffee together with a plate of sweet biscuits. The schnapps arrived minus the third glass.

'Salute' Miranda whispered touching her glass to mine.

'Down the hatch,' I murmured, Franz and Carlotta had disappeared silently. We drank our coffee quietly, brown eyes searching blue.

'Tomas,' she said using the Portuguese accent on my name, 'we have a word in our language it is simpatico, it means to connect with someone, to understand them, to be their friend, Tomas we have simpatico you and I, and now it is time to sleep.'

Tip toeing quietly up the stairs Miranda took me to a small bedroom with a single bed covered with a patchwork quilt. The room glowed softly from an outside street lamp; her perfume haunted the air. Without switching on the light she kissed me deeply and fumbled at my shirt buttons. We undressed one another gently and side by side on the bed staring into one and others eyes. My first embrace was fierce, 'Softly Tomas, gently and slowly there is no hurry,' she said pushing me onto my back. Her lips and tongue caressed my nipples, I gasped when she moved further down, 'Oh my!' Miranda exclaimed, squirmed around and wriggled underneath me; I needed no further coaching and buried my face in her glory.

In the early hours it rained heavily beating on the shutters of our tiny paradise at the top of the hotel. I rose gently so as not to awaken Miranda, she stirred, her eyes caressed me, 'animal' she murmured and returned to her slumbers. I dressed and tiptoed through the foyer. My taxi swished quietly through shining streets. Handing the driver a couple of U.S. dollars I climbed quickly up the gangway. In our cabin Chester snored quietly his knees drawn up in a foetal position. Gathering up my toilet bag and towel I quickly showered and shaved. Back in the cabin I shook Chester awake, 'Come on sunshine on your feet, time to rise, the skipper wants his breakfast.'

'Where the bloody hell have you been man, Mac and Guinea are going spare they thought you had been mugged and rolled, and why have you got that stupid look on your dial? You look as happy as a pig in mud.'

'Chester I'm in love, I've met a girl that would knock your socks off.'

'Does she have a friend?'

'Not for you mate, look at the state of you; come on get a move on, anyway she is flying out to Jamaica tomorrow.'

'Flying, what is she a bloody witch or an angel?'

'More like an angel, she is an airline stewardess.'

'Can I go with her; I'd like to see my relatives on that island?'

'You can go to the galley and get cooking mate, Winston don't like you malingering.'

'Malingering, what's that when it's at home? Guinea will give you malingering when he sees you, and so will old Hopalong.' Strangely enough the chief steward totally ignored me and at morning "smoko," Mac and Guinea each gave me a knowing leer.

'You crafty bastard, the barman told us all about that bird you picked up, air hostie my butt.'

43

'You'd better believe it my son, worth jumping ship for that one. She is flying out early Tuesday morning and I wish I was going with her.'

'She's having you on mate, how much did it cost ya?'

'Absolutely nothing, she even paid her share of the dinner and the hotel confirmed that she works for Varig.'

'Bollocks!' yelled Guinea, 'who do you think you are Casa b***** nova?' Mac grinned from ear to ear, 'He looks like he fell down a drain and came up with a roast dinner.'

S.S *Barranca* stayed in Rio loading cargo for another week. During this time I went ashore only once to the market and purchased the butterfly wing tray for my mother. Forty years later it still sat in her parlour, resplendent and iridescent. The colour of the butterfly wings never faded and always reminded me of Rio and Miranda and the night I received a sexual education.

· · ···

The weeks came and went, the heat intensified, we sailed back on our tracks. I spent more leisure time in the seaman's mess than I did in my own. In conversation I learned that stewards in general were looked down on as a bunch of big girls, most of them, "Great galloping poufs," was the way Guinea put it. I seriously thought about changing departments for a while until I thought about the cold weather up north. *Barranca* chugged her way swiftly loading for home, Salvador, Recife, Belem, which sits more or less on the equator, and is a fair way up a jungle shrouded river. Once, whilst again sleeping on deck, I heard animal sounds to make the goose bumps rise, I would later swear that I heard a jaguar's roar that night. I rolled over and thought about Miranda.

Monty the saloon steward and captain's "Tiger", became very ill and was paid off in Belem. As a displaced British seaman he would be treated possibly cured of what ailed him and sent home on the first available fast ship. Royal Mail lines ran a passenger service to and from Brazil; he might get home first class. Much to my surprise, given our earlier encounters the skipper chose me to replace Monty with a resultant increase in pay and prestige. With my eighteenth birthday on the horizon I took this promotion very seriously. We took on a much older displaced seaman to replace me. He explained that he had gone down with some strange tropical disease a couple of months earlier. Of sallow complexion and a slightly Oriental cast of eye, he told me his name was Fred and he lived in Birmingham. He bore a strange resemblance to Peter Ustinov and was as queer as a three speed walking stick.

'Told ya so,' jeered Mac and Guinea peering through galley hatch.

Part Two
TRINIDAD & TOBAGO

The Port of Spain dockland is more at home to tourist liners and passenger ships than to rusty old tramp steamers. Therefore as a cargo vessel *Barranca* was shunted over to the far side of the deep-water harbour, a considerable distance from the main quay. At this wharf a small dredger and what appeared to be a salvage barge, a garbage scow, and two tugboats, all floated in a turgid oil-ringed filthy sludge. Battered oil drums, frayed rope ends and tattered hemp fenders all littered the dockside and scavenging seagulls squawked and fought over scraps. Beside me Guinea spat into the filthy water below us as we studied the shore side activity. The sky was streaked with high white clouds that did nothing to shield us from the heat that bounced off the wharf or helped the few wharfies that sheltered beneath tattered canvas awnings. Without shoes the deck would scorch the skin off your feet.

'Shite Hawks,' my friend Guinea said gazing at the circling gulls. 'Look at all that crap lying about and the state of the water. I guess the turning tide doesn't reach this far to float it out to sea. Some tropic island paradise this.'

'Hang on mate, take a look at this bloke coming up the gangway.'

'Oh boy, check out that hat, and what's that he's carrying?'

'Looks like a very old shoeshine boy to me,' added Mac approaching us with a grin.

The man, a huge smile on his dark visage waved to the three of us as he climbed the rattling rungs of the gangplank 'You guys look in need of a haircut,' he called out, the accent and manner jovial.

'Haircut!' exclaimed Guinea, 'you look as if you've come to polish shoes with that box.'

The hat in question is very smart; a low crowned black "topper", with a stiff curly brim.

'Have you come to take the skipper to the races?' I asked tongue-in-cheek.

This character with a haughty smile on his ebony face opened the wooden box which he carried by a leather strap; inside sat a full kit of gleaming scissors combs and razors laying in snug velvet compartments.

'Look mon, what for you make yourselves looks stupid? This ain't no polish box, this box make you look sexy, stylish, de gals they love you.'

Mac who wears his black wavy hair very long retorted, 'Don't need any help man; they love me the way I am.'

'Like hell you don't,' snapped Guinea. 'You look like a b***** great fairy with that lot down to yer shoulders.'

'You can't talk Guinea, that bloke who cut yours in Rio did you no favours,' came my rejoinder, 'let's all get a trim it might cheer the skipper up.'

The two tough young seamen looked at me with disgust, 'Tommy your promotion has gone to your head sunshine just because you're the skipper's "Tiger", don't get big ideas.'

The Trinidadian barber called for a chair or stool, 'Who's going first?' he queried.

'You'd better go Mac,' said Guinea 'it'll take hours to get through that lot.'

Later that evening the three of us freshly barbered by the man with the unlikely name of Horatio, ("but call me Horry,") had agreed to meet the barber at a nightclub called *Miramar* The taxi dropped us at the door around nine pm after we had stopped for a few rum and Cokes on the way, naturally we were in good form.

'The joint is jumping,' yelled Guinea above the rhythmic clamour of a steel band.

A steep flight of dimly lit stairs led us up through a bunch of tough looking characters that looked like pimps and bouncers into a room full of noise, smoke and people. And such people: black, white, yellow, brown, and brindle; short and tall, fat and thin, all laughing, dancing, singing and having a wonderful time. Many of the white people dancing looked a little stiff and I guessed they were passengers from the great white liner that lay at the main terminus. Horry danced his way over with a gorgeous Indian looking woman, all curves, with smiling carmine lips, and dark flashing eyes.

'About time you guys arrived, I've got a table full of gals just dying to meet you.'

'This bloke is definitely on commission,' whispered Mac.

'Don't you worry Mac, just watch your pocket and don't get suckered into buying the "ladies", Guinea warned with heavy sarcasm, 'anything but rum and Coke.' The three "ladies," a cross section of the races that lived on the island, an Indian, an African, and an Oriental, all smiled welcome with dark dancing eyes. We ate, we danced, and we drank, and flirted outrageously with every girl in the nightclub. The air was palpable with sweat, stale perfume, and testosterone.

Guinea's golden hair shone like a beacon in the smoke filled room. A strikingly handsome mulatto woman was teaching him how to move in a sliding rhythm from the hips, instead of jiving around as if he was at the Hammersmith Palais in London. The band, beating on old oil drums cut to various depths and painted in rainbow hues, thumped out an intoxicating rhythm.

Predictably, a thin Hispanic looking man with outrageously long side-whiskers accosted Guinea, his neck dripped with gold chains. 'Hey man, that's my woman you got there.'

'OK man you can have her back.'

Guinea expertly spun the pretty mulatto back at the angry looking man. Who grabbed her, and commenced to give her a hard time, his hands slashing at the fetid air.

'Hey you moron, she was only showing me the way you guys dance for Pete's sake.'

Anger suffused the man's face, the eyes glittered dangerously, and the lips became a thin slit. 'You call me a moron you English pig, I'll spill your guts all over the street.'

Now Guinea proved the shipboard rumour about his fighting prowess, he grabbed the pimp by the shirtfront and head butted him swiftly between the eyes. The creep never knew what hit him, he sagged half comatose.

'Outside you greasy bastard,' Guinea snarled between tight lips, his handsome face stretched on the bones with anger. Hauling the now shaking pimp by the neck, scattering chain links like golden snow, he threw him down the stairs and followed at a run. All hell broke out in the doorway, with bouncers and pimps trying to hamper Guinea. This gave the battered Latino time to gather his wits. Mac and I charged down after our incensed friend, pushing aside cursing spectators in our wake.

Disaster! Guinea lay on the filthy footpath with a knife protruding from his stomach. He lay curled into a foetal position, his legs jerking spasmodically, his hands clutching ineffectually at his gut.

Mac took off after the fleeing pimp.

'Somebody please call a ambulance,' I screamed in panic.

'It is too late Tommy,' Horatio murmured at my elbow, 'come we must now save your other friend.' Tugging my shirt he urged me to follow Mac.

Mac gave up the chase a couple of hundred yards down the street, as the slippery pimp disappeared down an embankment into the deep shadows of brush and scrub. Even in his rage Mac knew it would be folly to follow. The three of us trudged back to Miramar; police had cordoned off an area around Guinea's prostrate form. The once happy crowd, all now on the footpath, jostled for a glimpse of the wreck of what had once been a vibrant, life loving, hard working sailor man.

Tears streamed down my face as police shouted questions. Feet shuffled uncomfortably on the side walk. The sweating faces of the staring throng lit by red and blue neon appeared distorted like a scene from hell in the tropic night.

'B***** hell Mac how did this happen, he was only dancing for Pete's sake?'

Mac, stony faced, remained silent. His usually smiling handsome features shrouded in grief. A police sergeant, very efficient, took details. 'We know this bad man, his name is Rico Gonzales, and everything will be done to catch this murdering swine.'

Turning to another officer, he said, 'Take these men back to their ship.'

Horatio stood at the curb and waved us off, a sad smile in his eyes.

On the quayside at the foot of the ship's gangway another police car, it's red and blue lights strobing the darkness, awaited our return. In the captains cabin we gave statements to a police inspector. Captain Skinner sat at his desk grim faced, whilst a constable wrote laboriously in his notebook. It turned out that I was the only one of the two of us that could give an accurate description of the killer. Mac had been at the bar at the far end of the club when the altercation broke out.

'Tomorrow,' the inspector stated, 'you will have to come to head quarters and sign these official documents. We will send a car.'

We were summoned immediately to the bridge. 'Morgan,' Skinner ground out the name through gritted teeth, 'you attract trouble like a shark after blood get out of my sight and take care both of you, watch what you say to the crew. Go below get some sleep. We've not heard the last of this by a long chalk.'

Down on the main deck half the crew had gathered to hear all about the tragedy. Mac brushed them off with a curt word or two. He and Guinea had sailed out of the Pool of London together since they had first set foot on a ship's deck as boy ratings.

Dull with remorse and bleary eyed, I wandered through the dreary alleyways of *Barranca* cursing the day I'd joined this floating harbinger of violence. In addition I was forced to explain everything all over again to Chester, who naturally agog with curiosity, questioned me unmercifully. I needed to wash the slime of the night off my skin; I stood under a scalding shower for untold minutes. Towelling off I stared at myself in the mirror through bloodshot eyes. The face that stared back had aged;

deep creases of misery scoured my cheeks and drew shadows from nose to mouth and I no longer looked like the innocent youth that had signed on. Eventually I fell into a troubled sleep. The next morning staring into the mirror to shave the eyes that glared guiltily back accused; 'You should have stepped in at the top of the stairs and stopped your mate from going down, maybe he would still be alive.' The shadow of that look has haunted me ever since.

Next morning the Police Land Rover with a uniformed sergeant at the wheel drove Mac and me to the station house. The murdering pimp, already behind bars, glowered at us.

'That's the bastard,' I yelled!

My statement of events clearly impressed the inspector, a neat compact man with shrewd eyes, he advised me in a matter of fact tone, and 'Of course you will have to stay on the island to give evidence at the trial.'

'No way,' startled beyond belief I lifted my head from my neatly typed copy to stare at his serious face.

'Your positive identification is critical.'

'But what about my job we've already paid off one steward and a cook?'

'Do not worry, all will be arranged, accommodation, a replacement for you, we have a displaced seaman standing ready.'

Thereafter it was all arranged above my head. 'Hopalong' worked out the pay I was due, a little less than forty pounds Sterling around eighty U.S. dollars, and I found myself with suitcase packed at the gangway head.

'I wish I was you man,' a sad faced Chester gripped my hand. 'I'd do anything to get off this bastard of a ship. Now you learn all about this steel band business you hear and tell me all about it when you get back home?' Trust Chester to think of drums at a time like this. Mac tried hard to say goodbye but his throat would not function. Grabbing me by the elbows, he cleared his throat and said in strangled tones, 'Nail that murdering creep good and proper Morg and I'll see you when you get home. You've got my address, don't forget now, and write to me.'

My friend the bosun stepped forward and gripped my shoulders tight, 'Don't take all this too personal Tom, look after yourself and watch out for that prick's mates, this is a small island and there is bound to be some kind of come back when they know you are ashore and giving eye witness testimony.'

I had not thought of this and thanked him for the warning. He gave me a wink and the thumbs up. Chief Cassidy snotty to the last wished me a hypercritical fond farewell. 'Don't do anything I wouldn't do Morgan, and watch out for the clap.' Not another soul of the ship's complement was in sight except the first mate who gave an ironic salute from the foredeck.

The accommodation turned out to be at the Missions to Seamen. A religious order that ran these recreation and accommodation centres for merchant seamen in major ports and harbours around the world. A navy blue flag with a white flying angel in midfield flapped lazily above a double storey white stucco building. At the door, the police driver introduced me to a small elderly Padre who greeted me warmly.

'Thomas is a goodly biblical name; please do not doubt my sincerity young man when I say you are welcome in this place.' The irony was lost on me, 'make yourself at home, it may be a long stay, the jails are full of felons and the wheels of justice grind very slowly indeed.'

I followed his slight figure; his stooped shoulders seemed to be carrying the sins of the world. Up a flight of stairs he showed me to a room which although spacious, was exaggerated by a high white ceiling, white walls, and white bedspread, it was clean but sparsely furnished with a single bed, a chair, a small table, a small rug of subtle brown shadings, a crucifix and one small religious picture of the last supper the only decoration. Light streamed through a timber jalousie window creating bands of shadow that kept most of the heat out. I glanced out and looked onto a courtyard with one lonely palm tree in the centre. A small wardrobe was all that was provided for my few possessions. Never having been a religious person these austere surrounds seemed decidedly apt in the circumstances if somewhat depressing.

That evening a meal was provided in the canteen. A Dutch engineering officer, the only other resident greeted me cordially and we sat together for a dish of chicken and rice. I was to learn that chicken and rice turned up with monotonous regularity.

When darkness claimed my restless spirit I walked around and around the courtyard in a daze, my mind in turmoil. It seemed to me that the evil that stalked this planet, no matter where or when could not be relegated to chance. No, the threads of fortune were spun deep in our psyche. Why otherwise was I in this place? As sure as there are stars in the night sky it was ordained, a step into the future. That night was to be one of loneliest I had ever spent in my life and there have been a few. Two books were provided in the room, one the Bible, and the other a tattered paperback edition of W.B.Yeats poetry. A copy of which in later years became a constant companion on my travels. My favourite;

'HE WISHES FOR THE CLOTHS OF HEAVEN.'

Next morning after a very good breakfast, I sat in the sunny courtyard reading the local newspaper. 'Anybody here need a haircut or a shave?' A familiar voice enquired quietly from the shadows. Turning quickly I saw the welcome sight of Horatio's silly hat; beneath the hat a face full of chagrin offered a soothing balm to my troubled soul.

'Man I am so sorry about all this. That man is dangerous, and if he stays behind bars this town be a better place. Are you coping ok?'

'It's not your fault Horry, Guinea was a good friend and I am sad as all hell, but he was always a hothead. Guinea will be buried here at the Mission tomorrow.'

'I will come, and please Tommy, while you are here always talk with me, Port of Spain as you can see is a dangerous place.'

Next day the amazing "topper" came off at the graveside revealing a mass of tangled bushy curls streaked with a little grey. The service, given by the softly spoken Padre was attended only by Horatio me and the Dutch officer, who saluted the grave and hurried off, leaving the three of us in a forlorn little group.

The rum that Horry and I drank later that afternoon could not sooth away the sorrow. A lost incredibly numb feeling enshrouded me. I felt suspended in time as if this was not really happening. It seemed as if all that had occurred was observed by another from a great distance. Involved, but not involved. I seemed to be cushioned in a protective layer similar to fog or cotton wool. Try as I might the image of Guinea lying on the footpath was graven indelibly into my mind. Lonely night followed lonely night.

• • • • •

Almost two months passed, and still no date set for the trial. I had been away from home for five months. At home my family on hearing the news had sent messages of encouragement by way telegrams care of the shipping company and I had done likewise but could give them no reassurances as to my return.

The Padre had a lady who came in the office to take care of his record keeping and correspondence. A pleasant friendly woman in her late thirties Joan by name, always had a kind word and stayed for a chat with me. Joan had a very brisk almost brusque manner and favoured woollen twin sets and pearls in a very English way.

On a yet another sultry boring day she took me in her car to a swimming pool. The pool, behind a rock embankment, part of a smart hotel, enjoyed cooling sea breezes and had a small bar which furnished a drink called Planters Punch made with white rum. The view across the bay was not very inspiring as Trinidad is a mainly flat island. However, the cooling breezes were to bring me back time and time again in order to escape the humidity. Swimming took on a new dimension three or four times a week I would plough up and down the pool, growing lean, fit and tanned. Time still hung heavily with nothing to do all day and still no date for the trial. My eighteenth birthday came in January, Horatio and I got drunk.

February came and with it Carnival.

Carnival is the biggest celebration of the year. This pre Lenten festival lasts for forty-eight hours, and the people of Trinidad and Tobago really look forward to it as in the same way a European may anticipate Christmas. Steel bands have an enormous following in the communities and at Carnival each band chooses a theme for a fancy dress costume that their followers will wear for the celebrations. The costumes can depict an historical story, an event of note, or topics of current interest. The bands with their cut down and tuned forty-four gallon steel drums slung on straps around their necks practice night and day. Some enterprising drummers with a large full size forty-four gallon "pan", will wheel it on a special bogey pulled by admiring followers. In my Carnival year of 1958, I saw Roman soldiers in kilts of steel and helmets of iron, actually made from papier-mâché and aluminium foil and modern day

G.Is, marching in full jungle fatigues. Behind them came a swarm of young dancers clad in ballet tights and tutus with 'The Nutcracker' being gently played on small drums, behold Swan Lake! There followed a float with a band of school children playing on various instruments called 'Hot Jazz,' a student the very image of Louis Armstrong in a white suit led them blowing on a gleaming trumpet.

The costumes, very close to authentic and dazzling, are always applauded as they dance all the way from down town and up Main Street to The Savannah; a large sporting oval about a mile up town. Here all major sporting events are held, mainly cricket and horse racing. A street dance known as "chipping", a rhythmic shuffle, takes the crowds through the heat. Anything more energetic and they would all expire.

This pre Lenten orgy commences in the early morning and culminates in a spotlight parade around the racecourse circuit where each "band" with up to two or three hundred jumping, yelling, cavorting participants, awaits the judge's decision as to whom is going to win the year's grand prize. Points are awarded on costume design, the music and enthusiasm. As I panted my way around the dusty circuit I thought endurance and physical fitness also paid a huge part in the glittering result.

During my sojourn in Port of Spain, Horatio had dragged me from dockside bars, through drinking halls, dodgy night clubs, and everywhere we went Horry was treated to a raucous welcome and a great deal of respect. During these perambulations I met a horde of characters, some friendly, some distant, and some distinctly hostile. One man, a salvage diver of Polish descent who reminded me of Angus the bosun, became my particular mentor and constant companion. Mike, as the diver liked to be known, a man in his mid-thirties, blond, stocky and balding, was gregarious and well connected amongst the community. His high cheekbones and blue eyes spoke of his unmistakeable Slavic heritage.

We went to the more respectable nightclubs, watched Limbo dancers, listened to the latest calypso songs and "chipped" the shuffling dance of the islands. On one memorable occasion we ran into Horry in a nightclub who introduced us to a diminutive calypso singer who called himself 'Sparrow.' Through this introduction, we found ourselves involved in a 'Band' called Byzantine Glory. Sparrow was an inspiration to the steel band musicians. 'We're going to whip 'em this time,' was his constant call. The little guy had written a funky and lewd calypso called the "Garret Bounce"; this was to be their theme song. What it had to do with ancient Byzantium had me puzzled. The costumes the girls in the band wore left very little to the imagination although tended to illustrate the point of the lyric. Minimum coverage was the order of the day. They wore enormous headdresses, sequined bustier and panties of the same fabric. The men in tight leotards, with gleaming "armour" made from foil, carried fake spears, bows, arrows, and even musical instruments, such as lyres and huge brass horns of the period made from papier-mâché.

'Are you going to march with this mob?' Horry asked two days before the big day.

'You better believe it buddy,' was my enthusiastic reply. By this time totally caught up in the atmosphere, although not to the degree of donning a costume, I was determined to go the distance.

For the first three hours, with occasional stops for refreshment, Mike and I, always on the outskirts of the throng, "chipped' our way to the Savannah, and then around the race course, and waited breathlessly and exhausted for the judges verdict. The dust, the sweat, the insects caught in the bright lights, the swirling people, and the crackling atmospherics of the occasion had the two of us heading to the nearest bar as we waited for the result.

'Byzantine Glory', screamed the loud speakers.

'Oh ho ho', we yelled linking arms and dancing around in a crazy jig. Horatio as always was there with the band. 'You two', he called, 'this is going to be the greatest night of your miserable lives. Just you follow me and don't get lost.'

Thereafter it began again, the "chipping", out of the arena, down the main street to the dispersal point. Sweaty hugs and sloppy kisses were rained down on us as we paraded past the grandstand back onto the road and mercifully down hill to the cheers of a mainly drunken crowd.

'Now we go to the club,' this of course from Horatio.

'Oh no we don't Horry we have to eat and eat well,' said Mike, 'I want a steak, a bloody great big one, with fries and onions and lots of cold beer.'

'You know you white men got no stamina,' Horry laughed, 'see you there later.'

The cafe we chose to eat in was frequented by American troops from a base on the island. There was no way that the two of us, by now well known among the foreign nationals, could escape the hospitality of these marines, for the most part it would seem from the Southern States. When our New York sirloins arrived they filled half the plate, we fell to with gusto, beers kept coming supplied by the generous GIs.

'We know you Limeys never have any dough,' they laughed.

'I'm no Limey,' yelled Mike above the din of calypso singers occupying centre stage. One of the marines a top kick sergeant named "Bud" Costello yelled back, 'Oh that's right, sorry pal but Polacks come pretty close, you all just drink up, we got a shindig to go to, ya want to come?"

'You bet Sarg,' we chorused', what do we have to bring?'

'Why just your own selves Morg, we got all the booze and grub a man could possibly need pal, plus a few of the gals.' Financially I was suffering. Through the Royal Mail's agent in Port of Spain the British Seaman's Union paid me a pittance of six shillings a day. My forty dollars pay off was long gone. The generous American soldiers guessed at this and always took me under their wing on a night out.

We tumbled out into the street; introductions all round from Bud, Al and Bill and Joe and what all, far too many to remember. Sergeant Wayne "Bud" Costello from Biloxi had a "pad" just around the corner, which he and a couple of the other guys kept for their off camp rest and relaxation. Not that they ever did much out at the base. Costello a ruddy complexioned six-footer had respect from his squad of buddies as he taught unarmed combat at the base and was a physical fitness nut. Mike and I had bumped into him at a hotel which catered for the tourist trade. We had walked in for a late afternoon beer after a swim at the pool on the beach to find him at the bar throwing poker dice with the barman. Mike watched for a while and offered him a drink and they played dice for drinks half the night. We had been buddies ever since.

Outside the restaurant the other Marines had headed off and were well on their way around the corner. The trio of Mike, Wayne and I paused on the footpath while Mike lit up a cigarette. From out of the mid-night gloom four men obviously full of Carnival cheer approached in a laughing huddle.

'Rass mon, you one crazy mon,' the speaker pushed his friend gently on the shoulder who made a slurping noise through his teeth. 'You rass clart mon, don't push me.'

Then the group seemed to scatter in a haphazard fashion; they came at the three of us from different angles. One man raised a gleaming machete, used on the island for cutting sugarcane and known colloquially as a cutlass this was a favourite weapon of street gangs.

The "cutlass" man headed straight for me. Mike pushed me into a doorway and turned to defend himself. Costello already had the "cutlass" man in an arm lock. The man screamed and I heard his arm snap like a twig. Mike kicked another attacker in the groin and followed with a Karate chop to the back of the neck. All at once, the odds had shortened, and the remaining hoodlums ran off into the night.

It all happened so quickly I was left panting with an adrenaline rush.

'S*** what was that? You blokes really know how to handle yourselves, were they after money?'

"Cutlass" man lay groaning at Bud's feet, he knelt beside the cowering thug and seized a fist full of greasy dread locks. 'So', he whispered menacingly through gritted teeth, 'you are all crazy men to try this on Carnival night there are cops everywhere.'

'We told it was the best time,' the man groaned.

'Who told you that crap man?'

'Rico, Rico Gonzales that's who, he wants this man dead so he can't testify.'

He gestured at me where I stood in the doorway still shaking with reaction to the sudden attack. 'You are a dead man for sure honky.' All of a sudden the bosun's warning came flooding back.

The other assailant raising himself to his knees, blood oozing from a gash on his chin where it had hit the concrete, he glared at "Cutlass" man, 'Shut your stupid mouth mon.'

'Goddamn it to hell Tom,' Mike breathing heavily exclaimed, 'we've been wandering around this place like a couple of dumb tourists and all the time I should have known you would be a target for these pukes.'

Wayne chipped in with, 'From now on you watch your arse Morg, travel by taxi and never alone OK?'

'Hell guys I like this place but if I'm going to lose my life, I just want out.'

Costello rubbed his hands in washing action, 'We're wasting good drinking time on this scum, c'mon let's get to the party.'

'What about these characters,' I asked.

'Leave that trash where they lie in the gutter.'

'Shouldn't we call the police?'

'Nah Tommy, too much paperwork and bulls***, leave these pigs where they belong. They are gonna be in trouble from their own kind anyway.'

At the "pad", all was in full swing. Buddy Holly on the record player and girls, girls and more girls. Behind the bar, not bottles, but cases of Bourbon, Scotch, Bacardi, and Vodka, plus Budweiser on ice and Champagne for the girls. A barman obviously hired for the occasion presided over the "doins", as Wayne called them. A smorgasbord of food lay on a cloth spread long table.

'You blokes don't stint yourselves, where does a soldier get all this stuff from Sarg?' I asked. Costello tapped his nose, 'What you don't know won't hurt you buddy, just enjoy'.

Off to one side, a woman standing all alone watched the swirling guests and dancers with an almost superior gaze. The music changed. A slow Latin beat eased the dancers into a hip-hugging shuffle. I noticed the hair, modishly cut, not quite blonde, and not quite red, it fell softly around a pointed chin, urchin like, and the features sharp the nose straight, pale skin on high cheek bones. I approached quietly; her green eyes measured me, acknowledged my approach.

'Would you like to dance?'

'I'll give you a try Tom Morgan.'

'How come you know my name?'

We slid easily into one another's arms. Her head barely reached my chin. 'This is a very small island Mr Morgan, and there are not many young eligible British bachelors available. You had better watch yourself.'

Her skin was alabaster white; a tiny ridge of freckles ran across her nose.

'So it is only fair that I know your name.'

'I'm Carolyn Harvey and it is Mrs but divorced. My friends call me Caz.'

We shuffled around for a while.

'Your perfume is a delight, what is it Mrs Harvey?' I could play snooty too.

'Schiaparelli, Italian, the best and very expensive Tom Morgan, duty free of course.'

Her voice was low, very English.

'So what are you doing here in Port of Spain?'

'Staying with my parents, doing absolutely nothing, just like you.'

'I wouldn't call being held against ones will to testify in a murder trial as nothing Mrs Harvey. One of my best friends was slaughtered by a jealous murdering pimp and I'm here to see the bastard hang.'

'I doubt that a hanging will occur you silly boy, his lawyers are pleading self defence and he will get five years, three with good behaviour.'

'What? That is insane, this bastard Rico provoked the whole thing, and Guinea was only dancing for Pete's sake. Anyway how do you know all this?'

'My father is with the consulate and has his ear to the ground.'

'Well you tell your father that earlier tonight a gang of cut-throats attacked Wayne, Mike and I, with the sole purpose of shutting me up.'

'So what happened, did you tell the police?'

'No.'

'Well more fool you, how did you know what their purpose was?'

'Costello scared the story out of one of them.'

'You had better be careful Tom; you're running around with a very dubious crowd.'

'Hey steady on, these people have befriended me and tonight Mike and Wayne saved my life.'

'O.K. so you like to run with the tough guys, just watch yourself Tom Morgan, my father has his eye on you.'

'So how come you're here tonight with all the wrong people?'

'I like to add a little hot chilli sauce to my otherwise very proper life, now dance Tom Morgan and shut up your mouth for a while.'

Her head fitted comfortably into my shoulder. We moved quietly for a few minutes. The room held an ambient glow, all the lights out except behind the bar and a couple of low gold shaded lamps. I could take a lot of this. Suddenly she pushed me away, and holding me at arms length, those green eyes flashed with pique.

'You are a real babe in the woods; you are either naive to the extreme, or completely stupid. Bud Costello smuggles liquor and cigars from Venezuela, and that mad treasure hunting Pole is only suffered by the authorities because he dives where no other man will go.'

'Thanks a lot, maybe you're right, I'm only eighteen going on nineteen, and you're a grown up woman of what twenty two or three, who knows it all.'

'Not at all Tom, I've been all kinds of a fool too, my kids live in London with their dolt of a father and I've run to Mummy and Daddy for help. I'm sorry I did not mean to disillusion you, the truth often hurts, but it must be told. You seem like a nice guy and I'd hate to see you hurt.'

'Don't worry I'm building quite a shell to hide in. May I call you Carolyn?'

'Don't you dare, my friends call me Caz.'

'Tough as old steel, it suits you.'

At that moment, the music changed. Little Richard charged out of the speaker with Boney Moroni and Long Tall Sally. We swung easily into a jive. Moving well together, we twisted and turned, rocking and rolling in perfect unison. The other dancers moved to give us room and applauded at the end.

Panting and sweating in the heat, we retired to the bar for cold drinks.

'Where did you learn to jive like that?'

'Frankly it was on Saturday nights at a local Youth Club with my favourite girl.' I replied, 'What about you?'

'The Streatham Locarno, we had a nice house near there when I was a teenager.'

'So what does your Daddy do at the Consulate?'

Caz shrugged her white shoulders.

'Oh some military thing; he went into the tank corps at the start of the last war, and came out a major with medals all over the shop. Who knows? I certainly don't. Like all the men who came back he never speaks of it. How about your folks back home?'

'Oh, there's just my mother, my sister, an aunt and a pest of a girl cousin, we all live together in a council house. Don't ask me what happened to the men in their lives it's Taboo to ask. Say how come you don't have a sun tan like the rest of us?'

'That was a quick change of subject. I hate the sun it brings me out in freckles all over.'

'I wouldn't mind joining the dots.'

'You are a cheeky and brash young man Tom Morgan.' However, I could see she did not seem to reject the idea totally. As if on cue Costello's ruddy face appeared above her left shoulder, 'Hey you two, picnic at the beach tomorrow, around lunchtime, are you on?'

'It is already tomorrow,' Caz pointed out with a waspish edge to her voice, 'and do not call me until sundown, goodnight.' Gathering up her wrap and handbag, she pecked us both on the cheek, 'my car will be waiting.'

Following her to the door I observed one of Battoo Brother's smart hire cars waiting. The driver jumped from the gleaming limo and opened the rear passenger door with a touch of his cap. The tall driver turned to where I stood mouth agape and gave me a knowing grin. This was obviously a regular occurrence.

'B***** hell she thinks she's royalty,' I muttered as I turned and rejoined the throng of seething bodies, smoke, and noise. I found Mike ensconced in a corner with two attractive girls.

'Hey Morg, take a pew this is Venus and this is Mai.'

Venus looked Indian and Mai Asian.

'You've got to be joking,' I snarled, angry at my loss of Caz and pissed off at her imperious goodnight. I knew that Venus and Mai worked as ground staff at the Pan-Am check in desk out at the airport and were ready willing and able. Totally exhausted and frustrated, all I wanted was my humble bed.

Awaking late next morning and missing breakfast, I sat in the courtyard with a stewed coffee and listened to the news over the speaker set on the wall. Apart from all the usual international guff, I learned that Sparrow had won the prize for the Calypso of the year with the "Garret Bounce." It would now be played and played on the local radio day and night until it drove everyone to distraction. Byzantine Glory and Sparrow had made a clean sweep of it. Horatio turned up around lunchtime drunk as a lord. The Padre took a very dim view of Carnival proceedings so I walked him down the street, poured coffee and food into him and sent him on his way rejoicing.

Around six p.m. whilst seriously considering a very early night I was called to the phone.

'Hello.'

'Hello yourself Tom Morgan,' a familiar high toned female voice replied, 'my father wishes to meet you in person. Be at the Collingwood Hotel at eight sharp. You know every bar in town so don't be late.'

'Your word is my command princess; do I wear a dinner jacket?'

'Do not get smart Morgan; just be there on time, the old man hates tardiness.'

This really amused me as the people on this island were so relaxed about time no one ever arrived at the appointed hour which infuriated most European ex pats.

'Listen Caz, I was about to turn in, you know, getting some beauty sleep.'

The waspish tone came with extra venom, 'Just get your arse down there.' Her tone brooked no refusal, and the phone clicked into silence.

At eight on the dot, I wandered in dressed casually as usual and went straight to the bar. The Collingwood Hotel, named after a famous British admiral, was festooned with pictures of sailing ships blowing one another out of the water. The flags, flying bravely at the mastheads, were mainly French and British, but a few Spanish and American dotted the canvases; the Union Jack always seemed to dominate. Collingwood, Nelson, Hood, Abercrombie, and various other seafaring luminaries glared down in bewigged and ruddy cheeked splendour at the members of Port of Spain society as they gathered for cocktails. Behind the copper topped bar Benjamin, immaculate in a white mess jacket, greeted me cordially with,

'Ah, ah, Mr Tom, long time no sees, is you having a punch?'

'No Ben, just a local beer will be fine thanks. Have you seen Mrs Harvey and her old man around?'

'Oh they be in the lounge Mr Tom, you want I bring your drink in there.'

'Yes Ben, but this once I'll take it in a glass thanks.' Ben rolled his eyes and muttered sotto voce, 'big time huh.'

I strolled casually into the lounge adjacent to the main dining room. Caz sat in a corner chair so that she could survey the whole room. Clad in a green shimmering frock of some expensive fabric, she gestured toward me. The man beside her stood, and offered his hand. Of medium build, ramrod straight, he had close cut thinning grey hair and a very military moustache plus the martial bearing to go with it; his hand shake cool and firm.

'Hello young fella me lad, what will you have to drink?'

'It's on its way thank you sir.' I said wishing I'd had a haircut.

'Jolly good take a pew, I'm Percy Gordon.'

His suit, an American washable lightweight, worn with casual elegance, sported a silk pocket-handkerchief and a regimental tie adorned his button down shirt. 'Now then young fella,' he began as soon as we were seated, 'we've got to keep you out of trouble. Carolyn told me of yesterdays adventures. Not good, definitely not good. From now on, you will be under constant surveillance; what is far more important you have far too much idle time. What would you say to a job while you wait for the trial which could be months away yet?'

'That would be extra good sir, I need some money to get by on.'

'Right this place needs an assistant manager, apart from your sea time what other experience do you have?'

Strangely, I had an eerie feeling that Percy already knew the answer. I told him of my twelve months in London's West End hotels, which included the Savoy, and the Hyde Park, where I had been selected to be the commis waiter who had served at a dinner for the Queen and Prince Phillip. As I recounted my history he cried,

'Well done, only the best young fella, b***** good show just the ticket!'

Rubbing his hands together he called for more drinks, and added,

'Benjamin, fetch Mr Morris would you, there's a good chap?'

Morris bustled in, 'Anything wrong Mr Gordon?' A prominent Welsh accent and a servile rubbing of the hands betrayed a nervous disposition.

'No, no, no, old chap, meet Tom Morgan. Welsh name but not one of your countrymen, ha, ha, Thomas, speak up like a good lad. Tell Morris here all about yourself.'

Feeling slightly patronised I did so and found myself hired at full bed and board and two hundred U.S. dollars a month. Totally astounded I worked out that I would get about twenty-five pounds Sterling a week, a months pay in the Merchant Marine.

'Do not worry about the work permit, visa and so on old man,' Percy told Morris, 'I'll fix all that with the authorities.' then turning and fixing me with a stern eye he said, 'Now then Thomas stay on this property as much as possible, if you have to go out travel by taxi, and try to have a chum with you' no gallivanting with those scallywags you've picked up on your travels.'

'Sir they are my friends, good men.'

'Good in a fight or in a bar Tom, but that activity is not good for your long term welfare. Do we understand one another?'

'C'mon Dad let's eat I'm starved,' Caz interrupted quickly before I could defend my friends again and winked at me, successfully fielding a reply that I later may have regretted. Over a very good dinner, we discussed the elections coming up in the US, Castro and Cuba, Elvis, and just about every thing under the sun. The other tables filled up with ex-pats who all seemed to know good old Percy. However there was a look of steel in his eye, as he and Caz were leaving he shook my hand in a firm grip and said,

'Do not let me down young fella me lad, or I'll have your guts for garters.' Caz smiled sweetly as her father left the room with a handshake here and a clap on the shoulder there of a few diners as he passed through the tables.

'A thank you Caz would be nice Thomas,' her look was inviting, 'and now I know exactly where to find you.'

'Don't count on it, but thank your old man, he is the last of a vanishing breed.'

Thereafter, Thomas J Morgan found himself housed in a small but comfortable air-conditioned room at one of Trinidad's more fashionable hotels. Morris introduced me to the staff and briefed me on my duties. Nothing very onerous required I just had to be there when Morris was not, fill in as barman between Ben's shifts, and watch the checking in desk. The manager had a wife, who put on a few airs and graces and floated about looking important. It was a pleasant occupation, except for the long hours.

Many of the 'house guests' tended to be American, Canadian, or British tourists, who stayed one or two nights and then flew on. The regulars, for the most part third and fourth generation planters and professionals, treated me cordially.

The small bar that Benjamin presided over had a dartboard. Whilst in long off duty hours at sea, I had practiced and played the game to while away the monotonous hours. Therefore I was a very good shot with the old "arrows". Very soon the regulars would challenge me to a match and

I became a favourite with many a laugh and comments about a misspent youth.

Several of these wealthy customers came once or twice a week to eat breakfast, quite often with the shakes from over indulgence the night before. As the staff on duty only served meals, it fell to me to open the bar and pour a stiff brandy into their morning coffee.

One of these patrons, an American with the good old boy name of Hank, obviously a committed alcoholic, became more regular than usual. Hank had once been tall, but now over weight and stooped; he observed the world through bloodshot, pale, washed out eyes. Grey of face with broken veins and a long nose that supported rimless specs he surprised me with a suggestion that I might like to see more of the island.

"I'm leaving in a couple of days to go down to my ranch and pay the workers. Do you feel like a trip?"

Morris agreed to let me go, and two days later I found himself in an air-conditioned Cadillac bumping and swaying over country roads. Thankfully Hank had a driver, the booze he had consumed at breakfast hung like a ripe brandy cloud in the car. The actual trip was monotonous, nothing but sugar cane and banana trees on either side of a rutted potholed strip of bitumen that caused the big car to sway and dip like a ship at sea.

Pay day at the 'Ranch', as Hank called it took hours. Lines of workers queued in the humid afternoon. Two supervisors sat at a camp table and handed out the bright red local currency. Hank and I sat on cane chairs under a porch that shaded the office steps. By early evening, I had consumed too much cold local beer, and after the traditional chicken and rice supper, I fell asleep on a truckle cot provided by Hank in the rear of the office space.

The next day it rained in torrents just after we left the plantation, solid sheets of water that obliterated the narrow road, causing us to pull over onto the gravel shoulders for fear of hitting a vehicle coming the other way. The return trip took forever and poor old Hank had the shakes terribly. We stopped at a swampy crossroads, whilst the driver ran into a shack built from banana tree leaves and corrugated iron and there purchased a bottle of rum. Hank knocked it back like water all the way back to Port o' Spain. Just before we reached the city Hank invited me to his club for dinner. It was just called "The Key Club". The interior was sumptuous, moody lighting, way out modern furnishings, discrete booths. Hank said he would put me up for membership; one of his regular drinking buddies would go second for me. All I had to do was come up with $500 membership fee and $250 a year. I had as much chance of getting the dough as flying to the moon on Apollo with the rocket guys. I thanked him for the compliment anyway.

March came in with warmer weather. The rains still hammered down but not with such regularity. Some of the Marines started to call in. I despaired of their attempts to throw darts. They held and heaved them like javelins. Old Morris was not pleased at the noise they made and made it very obvious. They stopped coming. Mike and Horatio put in the rare appearance. Carolyn "Caz" Harvey became a regular, sitting neatly at the bar drinking G& T's or Planters Punch. We played darts and shared jokes and memories of London together.

One day, right out of the blue, she asked,

'How would you like to see Tobago?'

I knew that it was a tiny and beautiful island off the coast to the north.

'I'm flying over to Tobago and on to Granada for a three day break. Do you think you can make it?'

'I doubt it; Morris keeps a close reign on me, due to your father's urging.'

'Leave it to me handsome,' she said hopping off the stool and heading for Morris's office. I had never thought of myself as handsome, but I guess I had something the girls liked.

'All set,' she gave me a cheeky grin, 'be ready by nine o clock sharp, I'll pick you up.'

On Friday, promptly at nine in the am I waited on the front steps. Dressed in neatly pressed grey worsted trousers with a pale blue short sleeved shirt and polished black loafers. I carried a change of clothes in a small bag, two more shirts, a tie, and a change of underwear. The tie in case we went somewhere formal, one never knew on these tourist islands. Caz arrived the regulatory ten minutes late in a taxi looking cool and elegant in a cream sun dress she wound down the window and called, 'Jump in Morgan it's a long drive to the air strip.'

Thankfully, the cab was a huge white comfortable air-conditioned Chevy, for it took almost an hour to get to the strip. The aerodrome turned out to be an aviation club with a dozen or more small brightly-coloured light aircraft scattered about. The pilot greeted us in the small timbered clubhouse.

'Bang on time old girl,' he chortled, 'the kite is full of juice and all warmed up.'

'Tom Morgan thus is Brian Wright, take no notice of his RAF slang he's OK?'

The little aircraft, painted a bright red and white was ready and waiting and we headed south, the panoramic views of the island spread out below took my breath away, then turning in a north easterly direction we headed for Tobago. Having never flown in any kind of aeroplane before I held on grimly to the seat, Carolyn smiling at my nervousness took my hand in hers.

The coastline was dotted with tiny coves with palm trees almost to the shoreline, white sandy crescents hidden behind acres of sugar cane or banana trees, the hinterland was an intense jumble of intense green plantations, pierced here and there by low jungle clad hills. Away on the southwest, the mighty asphalt lake with adjacent buildings and workshops blotted an otherwise pristine landscape. Here and there one or two small towns peaked from beneath the greenest of green foliage. Port of Spain the obvious capitol loomed large, with a cruise ship in the dock. Swinging north we flew over the American base at Shagaramas, and on over the narrow strip of ocean that separated the two islands. The journey took less time than the drive to the airstrip. Settling into a gentle approach Brian set the 'plane down smooth and easy, she took my hand again, noting that I was a little pale of face.

'There's a first time for everything,' she whispered.

'Righto you two, off you get I'll be back at 1500 hours tomorrow. We are due in Granada at 1800, flight plan all sorted so don't be late.'

Caz reached across and patted Brian on the shoulder, 'you're a pain in the arse Brian with all your toddle pip, but you're a real pal, see you tomorrow.'

A wind of around 10-12 knots stirred the surrounding palms and the windsock stood out almost due west. A short taxi into the wind and the little 'plane was up and away. I gathered up our bags and headed toward the only building in sight, a long low bungalow construction which blended with the surrounds.

Caz had told me that this was the Hotel Eden. The path of gravel and crushed shell led to a veranda that ran the entire length of a long low timber building situated on a small knoll. I could hear the pounding of waves but could not see a beach through the surrounding palms elephant ears and banana trees. The manicured garden was filled with blooming bougainvilleas, frangipani and colourful shrubs and with flowers of all the colours of the rainbow that gave off a heavenly perfume. Three steps led us to the double entrance, the doors flanked on either side by large tubs of elegantly drooping orchids. My senses swam in the exotic fragrant air; 'Wow!' was all I could say. 'Wait 'til you get inside,' she laughed taking me by the arm.

The entrance led into a lobby set under a high truss ceiling that followed the roofline and was lined with rattan over enormous exposed beams, beneath which pendant fans turned lazily. The highly polished timber floor was scattered with what looked like woven Mexican rugs. Palms in pots sat beside clusters of leather furniture adding to a warmly welcoming scene. No formal reception area dominated, just a beautiful antique desk behind which sat a man dressed in tropical whites. Rising to greet us he took Caz by both hands like an old friend.

'Caz, how wonderful to see you, how is your dear father?'

'Same as always,' this with that cheeky grin, 'Peter Squires meet Tom Morgan.'

We shook hands, Peter eyeing me in an inquiring manner but only saying in a very British voice, 'Welcome, welcome, lunch will be served soon, what about a drink first?'

Squires a tall thin man, deeply tanned, had sun streaked blond hair with touches of grey, a schoolboy lock fell over his forehead giving him a youthful appearance, he led us across the foyer to a discreet door set in the far wall.

So far, I had not seen a single sign that told me that this was a hotel.

Nevertheless, if the name was 'Eden' it came very close to the real thing to my thinking. The cocktail lounge, small and intimate, streaked with sunshine and shadow from tall windows fitted with jalousie shutters, had a long bar of split bamboo topped with a slab of deep red hardwood polished to a high sheen behind which a bar steward dressed in an immaculate red mess jacket greeted us with a salaam. The man of obvious Indian descent asked their pleasure in a soft whisper.

'Gin and tonics I think ok with you two?'

'Perfect,' Caz confirmed. The drinks arrived with a menu on which Tom observed the name of the hotel for the first time.

'Thoroughly recommend the curry, all my staff are third or fourth generation Indian and they know their stuff.'

I knew the history of Indian workers brought out by the planters to fill a huge gap in the workforce in the 1800s. Of course they had multiplied and by dint of hard work had risen to be the virtual 'middle class' of the islands.

Lunch was served in a nook on the veranda sheltered from the prevailing wind. I could now see the ocean through the swaying palms. Never in all my dreams would I have aspired to this paradise. My memory took me back twelve months or more to the time when the old *Barranca* sailed past these islands heading for Brazil with an innocent pantry boy looking expectantly toward his first view of the tropics. To our right and slightly behind us a ridge of low verdant hills became shrouded in a misty rain shower that lasted less than a minute, causing a small rainbow to arc across to the beach.

We ate the excellent curry in companionable silence. It would seem that we were alone in the hotel, except for a couple I spotted dressed in colourful shirts and Bermuda shorts down on the beach. It was off-season for the wealthy tourists from America and Canada that habitually came down during the northern months of January and February.

After lunch the rain had set in for good, which put a real damper on exploring. My host suggested a shower and a siesta gladly accepted by me, now full of good food and exhausted by all the new sites and sensations. Carefully hanging my shirts and trousers, I then took a long warm shower and climbed beneath the mosquito net shroud.

71

I slept until five o' clock, dressed, and wandered down to the lobby. Peter sat at his beautiful desk fiddling with some papers and looking totally bored. Flicking back the hair that fell across his right eye in a practiced swoop of the head, he greeted me warmly,

'Hello chum, it's early for a drink and too late for tea. How about a hand of cards, do you play cribbage by any chance?'

Long boring hours at sea in the mess with nothing else to do had made me into a fair hand at crib. Cautiously I replied, 'a little, at least I know the rules.'

'Oh splendid, good show, I can't leave the phone so we shall play here if that is o.k.?' That is how Caz found us an hour later.

'Fifteen two, fifteen four, six for a run, and one for his knob, Tom you crafty bastard you win again. Hang on I'll tot up the points, that's almost five dollars I owe you good job we were only playing for five cents a point.'

'You two look as thick as thieves over there, what's going on?'

'Tom's giving me a lesson in the art of cribbage.'

'Really Thomas more signs of your misspent youth,' she noted with an arched eyebrow and a tiny smile, 'I wonder what else you have up your sleeve?'

I gave her a long appreciative look. I had never seen her so lovely. Her hair had been brushed until it glowed; she rarely used much make up and tonight her classic beauty shone. A gown of deep green showed off her figure. Peter and I stood and stared in admiration

'Your mouths are open like a pair of country yokels. Sundowners, I think boys.'

Taking one on each side of her by the arm she carried us off like sheep to the bar. We all dined together in the nook, lobster thermidor, and fresh green salad, an excellent Chablis and crème caramel. Peter left us to our coffee and small cigars. A silver sliver of a moon illuminated the night sky, the soft susurration of wind and waves the only sounds. She took my hand, 'Thomas Morgan on such a romantic night I believe that I can teach you a few things that your misspent youth may not as yet have encountered.'

I barely dared move. I had known, some deep atavistic sense had told me that the mutual feelings of two young people separated from home, lonely, but surrounded by strangers, would result in a reaching, a searching for warmth. We had admired one another from afar for weeks, hardly daring to step over the line and now the time had come. I looked into her eyes darkened with deep and mysterious shadow; I uttered not a word. Our love making was delirious, almost savage. Caz seemed insatiable, her lips fondled my body in places that shocked, and she guided me into an abyss of eroticism. This aggressive passion entirely was opposite to the gentle hours with Miranda.

Next morning I found myself alone; Caz had, with proper consideration for our host removed to her own room. Showered and breakfasted I found a path that meandered down to the beach. Shoes in hand, I wandered through the shallows, with the warm Caribbean lapping and curling around my feet. My thoughts were mainly on 'Guinea', I replayed the voyage of the *Barranca* in my mind; the people, the places, the events that had brought me here to this time and place. I thought of my mother, back in London waiting patiently for my return; could I go back? No, oh God no, not to that life, but how to stay. After the trial I had to leave, the newly formed Federation of West Indian Islands wanted all the semi skilled jobs, (like mine), for their own folk. Only specialist workers were allowed to stay. Maybe 'good old Percy' would sponsor me. Again no, Caz was not resident and I did not fool myself, last night had been a release of passion, a passing emotion, nothing more. Not unless this passion would lead us into a deeper more meaningful relationship? No in Percy's world young men did not marry older women and what about her children. My dilemma was simple in order to become resident I needed money to buy a business and become an employer. Not going to happen any day soon.

Returning to my room, I showered the sand off, and knocked on Caz's door. No response, I knocked again, the barest murmur nothing more. I shrugged and went onto the veranda, ordering coffee I asked for a newspaper, it arrived, two days old; I had read it in Port of Spain. As the lazy morning passed I read the business columns and searched the businesses for sale looking for a small restaurant to check sale prices. Caz turned up just in time for lunch. Strangely, the glamour of the night before was absent. She yawned a good morning, gave me a peck on the cheek and called for a gin and tonic, she seemed bored and preoccupied.

'Well Thomas, what do you say to a quick swim before lunch?' No sign in her eyes of anything deeper than a swim.

After the swim we ate a leisurely lunch. At three in the afternoon Brian arrived on time and we flew to Grenada a tiny gem of an island. Another luxurious hotel, another night identical to the first, and then it was over. The word love never ventured past our lips. For Caz it was a release, some pleasure away from parental eyes, for me a lesson to file under 'foibles of human nature.'

Arriving back in Trinidad I felt strangely disoriented, the last forty-eight hours leaving me bemused and somehow unsettled. Caz seemed to retreat to another place and became distant. Dropping me from her hire car at the Collingwood and with a casual 'See you later Tom,' she was gone.

Morris pleased to see my return handed me an official looking envelope, carrying the old fashioned seal of the Governor of Trinidad. At long last the date of the trial. May the 10th, was still three months away. Caz and I went to the Hotel Normandie a couple of times to dine and dance. Frankly I was getting a little fed up with Calypso music, and a perilous back breaking dance under an ever lowering bar called the Limbo. I went to The Key Club a couple of times as a guest. I badly needed the recognition that membership here would bring.

On one spectacular night at the Normandie, full of rum and good spirits I asked if I could play the Conga drum. The lessons I had received from my old friend Chester, the galley boy came to my aid, to my surprise everyone applauded, and the French owner of the hotel came to our table and offered us a drink. Andre the proprietor knew whom we were of course and in conversation he slipped in a warning. 'My young friends, you must take care, especially you Mrs Harvey, your father is not pleased with this romance and he is very powerful man.'

'My father is an old fashioned stick in the mud.'

'Maybe so Miss Carolyn but he pays your bills, after the trial I think he will terminate this affair with a stroke of the pen.' Coming down out of my exuberant mood, I realised the man was right. The British Consulate must know of my every move.

'A great pity young man, I could have used you here in this hotel. All my management team are European. They have comfortable quarters and excellent pay.'

Maybe, just maybe this was the answer to my dilemma, if I could swing it for a visa renewal; I could work here where the big dollars were.

Andre gave a very Gallic shrug and fixed me with a twinkle in his eyes, 'But still you have had a very educational experience no?'

Caz and I stared at one another with the sudden realisation the whole of society on the island must have knowledge of our affair, stupid to think otherwise. 'My old man will have been having kittens,' she giggled behind her hand, 'seducing a much younger man will be high on his list of naughties.'

We went to bed that night and made love as if there was no tomorrow.

Bud Costello, whom I had not seen in a month, came to the Collingwood on a quiet night. We sat in the garden with beers and I told him that I feared that I would be gone from the island as soon as the trial was over. 'I want to stay Bud, once this arsehole Rico is behind bars I think I would like to buy a little business, maybe a little bistro style café. My problem is the dough to invest in this.'

'You know Tommy I could help you, we could be partners, I reckon you would be good, with more tourists arriving every year and the locals looking for something other than the hotels we could do all right. I've heard from a reliable source that the Hilton Hotel Group are coming, this place will burst wide open. You do the work I'll put up the cash. When my time as a "jar head" is over I could come down a couple of times a year, pick up my cut and have a free vacation. There is one other thing, I trust you and I need a hand on a little enterprise I run, the money is good and it only takes a few hours of your R&R time.'

· · · · ·

The mango swamp was alive with mosquitoes; they stuck in swarms on my sweat streaked face. The evil smelling stuff I had smeared on did little to help. Costello crouched ahead of me in the boat, there was no moon, and I could feel his body heat and smell sweat and fear in the half cabin of our fifteen foot Haynes. The two black crewmen were under the stern thwarts, the whites of their eyes luminous in the meagre light through the shinny leaves. Summer sheet lightning flickered and I hoped the low cloud cover would open up with a downpour to camouflage our retreat from this pestilential coast.

Throbbing outboard engines crept ever closer to our hiding place. Searchlights flashed glittering spears of silver brightness, a kaleidoscope of black tree trunks and foliage. We held our breath; a lump the size of a fist blocked my throat, my heart thumped so loudly I was sure it would give us away. Something flopped in the murky water. Slowly, agonising so, the Coast Guard cutter eased past. We waited two more hours. Daylight came at 0530 and we had to be gone.

Running back under full throttle of our twin Mercury outboards Bud and I laughed like maniacs as the adrenalin settled in our veins. Our cargo of quality scotch and American cigarettes safe in the tiny hold watched over by one of the crew. We thumped our way across an easy swell; our landfall was at good old Hank's plantation. As dawn crept stealthily across the banana leaves we watched our two crewmen unload swiftly onto a jitney that carried the goods to a barn where Hank stood waiting. His khakis were freshly starched his face tight and eyes clear as blue crystal. This was a different man to the drunk I knew. Hank's lips twitched and he offered his hand, 'Welcome aboard Morgan, how you like it? You just made enough dough to pay your way into the club, three or four more trips and you've got the deposit on your bistro.'

Looking across at Bud I gave a wry grin, 'That's until we get caught, this is no secret you know, the authorities have heard the whispers and those bastards over there shoot first and ask questions later, I reckon I'll pass, thanks anyway.'

Hank and Costello exchanged looks, 'It's not that easy Tom, you're new to our racket, how do you know about the whispers.'

'Leave it out Hank, every bar in town has these bottles on the shelves, no duty stickers, fags sold over the counter at half price, your man that sells to Morris is a bit obvious, it's only a matter of time. No thanks fellas, I have no desire to end up in the slammer with Rico, or with a bullet in my back over the channel.'

Bud Costello drove me back to the hotel; we sat quietly in the Chevy listening to the tick of the engine cooling. 'Too bad Tommy, I reckon we'd have made a great team you're a stand up guy for a limey.' He gave me fifteen hundred US dollars.

· · · · ·

The courthouse stirred as one as I entered the witness box; a hush descended on the crowd that filled the place to capacity. In the front row good old Percy sat scowling up at me with his mischievous daughter beside him, next sat Morris and his wife, and behind them, Horatio, Mike, Bud Costello and some of the guys. The atmosphere heavy, pungent with sweat and the assorted perfume of the ladies and aftershave of the men which the overhead fans did nothing to dispel. High windows let in beams of sunshine in which dust motes danced. The bright colours of the ladies of African blood relieved the drabness of the members of the legal profession. The timber in the high and elaborate benches where the judiciary sat glowed like honey.

A shard of sunlight, split by the bars of the cage where the offenders sat, highlighted their misery. Some six or seven black men chained at foot and wrist sat in disconsolate silence. Rico stood in the forefront a knowing sneer on his lips, his black and greasy locks shorn to the skull. Prison seemed to have had no effect on his cocky persona. He stared with a burning and passionate gaze directly at me as he took the Bible and swore the oath.

The lawyers read all the statements of evidence and asked the usual questions, blah, blah, until the defence lawyer rose to his feet and pointed directly at me and half turning to the bench with arm still outstretched cried,

'Your Honour, it is well known among the islands that merchant seamen behave outrageously when ashore, they inspire drunken brawls, licentiousness, and I suggest to you and the jury that this man is no different from the rest. I further suggest that my client was provoked by this man's so called friend. The deceased drunken thug provoked the defendant by treating his girlfriend in an outrageous manner before assaulting him physically, and throwing him down a flight of stairs. My client had every right to defend himself.'

The stern judge, a grey curly wig highlighting his shiny plump features, removed his spectacles and with an audible sigh asked, 'Mr Chalmers, do you stand in my court and denigrate the very mercantile endeavours that keep these islands solvent? Surely not all seamen are as you describe. What do we know of this unfortunate that lost his life? Please impart that which we do know and do not indulge in ambiguous rhetoric. This young man's behaviour has been exemplary whilst on this island.' He turned to the jury, 'the inflammatory comments from my learned colleague will, I am sure ladies and gentlemen of the jury, will be ignored.' I glanced at Bud, his face empty of emotion, however the eyes glistened. Mr Chalmers tugged at his black gown. He tried in every way he could to blacken Guinea's character in order to prove self defence.

Eventually the prosecution called me, I took the witness stand and swore the oath and I described the scene as I recalled it in simple straight forward terms. Prosecution seemed satisfied and turned me over to Mr Chalmers. He paused for effect,

'Is it not so Mr Morgan your so called friend had a reputation as a bully and drunkard?'

'I saw no evidence of that behaviour in the previous months of our voyage.'

'Well sir, I have here,' and he waved a piece of paper,' a copy of his discharge book which shows that on two previous occasions he was discharged with a Declined to Report notation from two other ships on which he served. Does that not indicate that the captains of those vessels considered him undesirable? In fact the SS *Barranca* was a ship that was known to carry a notorious crew.'

I fought to keep calm and answered, 'That is not true sir, she may be a beaten up old tub that finds it hard to sign on crew, but the men I knew were OK.'I glared back at that human dross Gonzales.

Proceedings went on in this vein until I could take no more. I shouted pointing fiercely at the defendant, 'That man is a murdering exploiter of girls, everyone knows it. My friend was merely dancing learning your island steps; he did nothing to provoke this pimp.'

The lawyer gave a small smile. 'I have before me depositions from shipmates of yours that state he went out of his way to prove how tough he was.'

'Bulls***! Sorry your Honour, but that is just hearsay, some weak so and so getting sneaky licks in when the man is down, and I mean six feet down.'

My anger seethed out of my mouth, bottled up emotions ripped through me like flame. I knew that my rage was exactly what this smooth operator desired. I tried desperately to control the righteous indignation, I was speechless with fury. The judge's gavel banged continuously, I had fallen into Chalmers trap.

'No further questions you Honour.' The smarmy git gathered his gown around his rotund frame and sat as if he had discovered the answer to all the problems of the world, a small self satisfied smile on his fat lips.

Prosecution went through the rigmarole of question and answer with me and Rico Gonzales. I could clearly see that Caz had been right; this trial was headed for an easy verdict of manslaughter, a deal had been made.

We all rose for the verdict; guilty of manslaughter; five years, time off for good behaviour, including that already spent in custody. 'Rubbish,' I cried, it meant that the killer would walk free in a little over two years.

'Silence in court, any more of that Morgan and I'll hold you in contempt.'

The judge banged his gavel. I looked down at my friends with tears in my eyes. Sympathetic shakes of the head from all except good old Percy who gave me very hard eyes indeed.

On the courthouse steps, a man I did not know stepped forward and offered his hand.

'Mr Morgan, my name is Rodriguez, Harbour Master; you are required to report to my office within twenty four hours to register as a displaced British seaman. We will secure you a berth on the first available vessel.'

I did not know whether to be happy or sad, turning to my friends, I held up my hands in a gesture of despair.

'C'mon you licentious sailor you,' Horatio laughed, 'we got some drinking to do, your friend will lay happy in his grave knowing you were with him to the end.'

'To tell you the truth Horatio I don't feel much like, (in the lawyer's words), carousing, thank you all guys for coming, but I think I'd rather just go for a swim.'

'Why don't we all go for a swim?' suggested Mike.

The pool by the sea with the small bar had never seen such hilarity. Determined to break me out of my melancholy there was much horseplay, a great splashing and diving, great gales of laughter. Moreover, it worked. Gradually I brightened and shrugging off my black mood joined in to a degree. Mike, who knew the harbour master, told me there was no way the situation could be changed. My gloom returned.

'They can't wait to get rid of me, what did I ever do except work hard? What's more the boss at the Normandie said he would have liked to employ me.'

'Tommy you are a child, Caz's father is behind it all he could renew your work permit with a word in the right ear, but you are breaking his code of honour by so obviously shacking up with his daughter.'

'Rubbish! It's just a game with her she is over twenty one' I admitted bitterly, 'there is nothing in it just sex and he will send her back to her husband and kids pretty quick I should think. Ah the hell with it all Mike, there is a lot more to the world than these islands. A week ago I'd have done almost anything to stay here with the gang, open a little bistro, now it's back to sea and a free trip home. Caz and I both knew it was a "fling", nothing more, it is over mate otherwise she would be here with us now if it were not.

I received nary a word from her 'highnesses'. I was smart enough not to pursue a lost cause. Within a week a ship that carried one hundred passengers and also had humidified cargo holds to carry bananas arrived in Port of Spain. I signed on as assistant steward, which meant I would get paid. The friends that I had made were on the Port of Spain dockside to bid me farewell, no sign of Mrs Carolyn Harvey.

The voyage to Southampton passed without incident. On my best behaviour and showing skill serving at table and also pleasing the passengers with easy banter and knowledge of the Islands I was asked by the headwaiter to return next voyage.

'Sorry chum, too many bad memories. I think I'll try the Pacific next trip.'

I had, counting my time on *Barranca* and on the island, been away from home for a little over two years. What a time it had been. Southampton was as grotty as I remembered and it was raining as usual, that annoying drizzle that buggers up picnics and trips to the seaside, that only the Brits stoically put up with. I had changed the dollars into Sterling with the ship's purser and with savings from my hotel salary and Bud's $1500 I had almost a thousand quid in my pocket. I hired a taxi and went all the way home in style.

Only a mother can tell at a glance the changes wrought in her child, she silently acknowledged that young master Thomas had gone down somewhere over the horizon. The butterfly tray, gladly accepted was given a place of honour and my nightly visit to the pub suffered in silence. A snap shot of Guinea, Mac and I seated in an unknown bar, was all I had to show for my transference from a wet behind the ears kid to a man with a lot of memories. I telephoned Mac's home, however he was at sea. All my old school chums seemed dull and boring, and Maureen was engaged to some soldier due out of his national conscription any day, she was welcome to the squaddie. It was not long then before my sea bag was packed, and I bade a fond farewell to the family.

FIFTY CIGARETTES FOR CHRISTMAS

On the 23rd day of December, a Saturday, with all the festive jollity in full swing and home for Christmas for the first time in three years I decided, after a couple of pints at the local, to go to the Wimbledon Palais de Dance for a listen to Ken Macintosh's big band. He had just recorded a hit single called 'The Creep'. Available only on 78rpm, after all it was the fifties, it was an orchestral piece featuring saxophones in a slow bluesy beat allowing a dance that encouraged young couples to get close and cuddly. As I recall it roared up the Melody Maker's top 10.

I sat in the rear of the dance hall with a beer in my fist enjoying the atmosphere tapping the 'winklepickers' to the rhythms and checking out the girls. Like all dance halls of the time lighting was minimal and the gleaming facets of the central rotating silver ball sent slivers of broken phosphorous sliding over the darkened interior. This place was huge, the band, a full twenty four-piece orchestra on a raised dais featured a male and female vocalist. There was a gallery above a sort of viewing lounge that wove its way around the arena and provided a voyeuristic eyrie of gloomy plush seating. Couples sat up there with ghostly faces watching the dancers below and having a quick snog. A large crowd of boys and girls and some Mums and Dads swirled around the polished boards. Unexpectedly an old schoolyard chum, Wally Burke (of all people yeh you got it), stood at my elbow he was wearing the fashionable 'Edwardian' style suit of the time.

'Home on leave are you Thomas me old son?'

'No you Berk, I'm still in the b***** Atlantic with a force 10 gale up my backside.' Daft bugger always was.

Wally gave a chuckle, 'you always were a joker Tommy.'

'And you always ask silly questions.'

'Any chance of getting me away in your lot,' was the next silly question. I served in the Merchant Marine as a humble steward much to the envy of most of my acquaintances. The so-called glamour of travel and a deep suntan all year round added to the romance. Basically I worked 12 hours a day 7 days a week for weeks on end in order to come home with the tan and a couple of hundred 'quid' in my pocket.

'Buzz off Wally, I'm enjoying the band and you wouldn't last five minutes in a row boat on the Thames never mind the Bay of Biscay.'

He sloped off with a dejected droop of his narrow shoulders, the back of his thick flaxen hair combed into a DA fell over his collar and with a last turn of his pale snub nosed face he gave me the 'V' sign, definitely not for victory. Poor old Wal at eighteen and National Service call up age, the only reason he wanted to go to sea was to avoid the army making a man of him.

Then I saw her: dressed in a white sheath dress that showed a neat figure she danced with another girl. There were a great many men and young lads scattered around the dance floor, however they were mostly too worried about getting a knock back to ask for a dance. From a distance I watched the grace with which she executed the twirls and under arm dips of the 'jive' number.

Finishing my beer I moved down to the edge of the polished dance floor. Catching her eye I gave her one of the old what about it look, her little smile was enough.

'May I cut in?' The grimace from her chum would have frozen the whole of South London. In a trice we were together, her style was just like mine and we fit like professionals. The music which was in the last bracket for the night changed to the last but one dance and of course it was 'The Creep'. Macintosh had saved his big hit to almost the end. This is more a stylised shuffle than a dance definitely aimed at the "wallflowers", shy people male and female that stood around all night hoping for a miracle that would bring them instant romance.

The traditional last waltz followed, we nestled closer, her hair, vaguely blonde was as stiff as a board with lacquer. We exchanged names hers was Trudy.

'Where do you live?' This was a standard last dance question.

'Not far'. Was her standard last dance answer.

'Can I take you home or maybe go for a coffee?'

'Coffee sounds good.'

I knew a late night café nearby the usual 'greasy spoon'. We sat with the drunks and the maudlin with the steam and smell of rancid fat creating a cosy feeling and when four noisy louts swaggered in I said,

'Come on let's get out of here, do we need a taxi?'

'No we are nearly there already.'

The cold air of a December night sent ghostly trails of moisture from our mouths as with her arm tucked under mine we went silently on our way. Less than fifteen minutes later we arrived at a semi-detached villa set behind a small garden with a withered lawn and a border of rose bushes looking grimy and neglected. The entry hall light illuminated the mock lead light window set into the front door.

In the harsh light of the café the planes of her long face with too much make up, had seemed less romantic than under the seductive lighting of the dance hall. At the door her willing lips searching for a goodnight kiss took on a dangerous meaning. Trudy was very lonely, and obviously needed a fella but in the time honoured tradition she murmured,

'Mum will be waiting up for me.' With relief I set off on the long walk home. However we had exchanged phone numbers.

At around nine thirty on Christmas morning as I settled in for another hour kip the 'phone jangled me into full alert. Worried that it would awaken the sleeping mother who'd had a glass or two of port and lemon, "just for Christmas dear", I hurried down to the hall.

'Who is ringing at this hour on Christmas Day?' I growled. 'It's me,' a female voice. 'Ah Trudy, Merry Christmas to you, sorry about that, thought it might have been one of my stupid mates.' Not that there were that many, after having been at sea for a few years I had become tired of their parochial ways.

'Can we meet?'

'You live a couple of miles away and there are no buses today.'

'You walk my way, I'll walk your way and we can meet half way.'

'What for Trudy love? My family are all coming around for a big nosh and a "knees up" you know the sort of thing.'

'I've got a present for you.'

For me, why the heck would she buy me a gift? Then the 'penny dropped'.

Trudy like many other lonely teenagers was searching for a magic light to shine on a miserable suburban life, a way to escape the dreaded nine until five drudgery. Not that I blamed anyone for that after all that is what prompted me to join the Merchant Navy. Reluctantly I trudged through silent near freezing streets wishing I were back in bed, everyone else seemed to be.

We met and stood clumsily looking for words. Trudy mumbled, 'Merry Christmas Tommy,' lifting her face for a kiss she gave me fifty Senior Service cigarettes in a fancy box; I stammered my thanks feeling a total fraud for I knew we would never meet again. 'Will I see you tomorrow Tom?' I decided to be straight with her, 'Look love I sail on a three month cruise next Wednesday this is not a good idea. I'm a career seaman, I'll never come ashore, least ways not in London, and so it would be a lonely life for any girl to become attached to me. OK?'

The last I saw of the eager Trudy was the back of her hooded red raincoat as she walked slowly down the silent street of broken paving slabs. Passing St Mark's churchyard with its overgrown and forlorn cemetery she turned, waved, and then moved away into the misty morning sunlight.

I walked home passed the old Majestic cinema with its superb sweeping marble staircase now a Bingo Hall two days a week, the streets still empty except for the odd vehicle. The family were all astir, my young sister on her knees groping for her presents under the Christmas tree. I gave Mum the cigarettes, I still had plenty of duty frees. Around noon aunts and uncles cousins and neighbours drifted in. As usual all us men headed for the local pub while the women filled the table with cakes and mince pies and dressed it up with gaudy crackers and baubles all the while sipping on sherry or stout before putting two large capons in the oven. Our immediate neighbour baked the vegetables and Aunty Win set her homemade plum puddings on the stove.

Around three p.m. we staggered home with rosy cheeks from the cold and booze.

Laughter rang around the room as we all tucked into steaming plates of festive fare. After the meal Uncle George our annual Santa gave out the presents, we all pitched in to clear up and the nonsense began. Mistletoe hung above the door and all the uncles tried to manoeuvre

Aunty Eileen under it for a kiss, she was a statuesque red-haired beauty with a willing laugh. Our new radiogram belted out Frankie Lane, Johnny Ray, and Guy Mitchell. The room was too small to dance but all joined in the choruses. By eight all had gone home and I slept in the deep blue armchair that Grandad had left Mum in his will.

Three days later, Trudy forgotten, I rejoined my ship. A Federal Line refrigerated cargo carrier she took me cruising for several months to the sunny shores of Australia and New Zealand.

Part Three

AUSTRALIA AND NEW ZEALAND

Thereafter, a wiser seafarer now, I went to the offices of a prestigious shipping company, rather than the Shipping Federation's 'Pool'. No more rusty old tramps for this hoary old salt. Out of sheer luck, I was taken up immediately on a recently launched cargo passenger vessel of 7000 tons. Pride of the fleet: her captain was the Commodore, and I was to be his personal steward. The certificates of discharge in my seaman's identity book all read 'very good', and my hotel experience was noted; as the Commodore entertained lavishly in port my skill with the etiquette of social life would be useful.

Once again, I lugged my heavy suitcases across London to the King George V docks. The rain was coming down in its usual fashion driven slantwise by a chilling north wind. My taxi drew up on the wharf in a late afternoon gloom. Even in the sodden miasma of dockside stink my new vessel looked smart; her hull painted a light grey with white boot topping, she had a single oval shaped funnel slightly raked and painted a shining crimson with two black hoops. It towered over the bright white paint of the substantial midships housing, Swan and Edgar's ship building yards had turned out a real beauty.

At the top of the gangway, a Master at Arms in full uniform greeted me with,

'Do you have business aboard this ship sir?'

'Yes chief, joining as captain's steward.'

'The old man will be pleased to see you and no mistake, report to Mr Evans, Chief Steward right away, second door down first cabin on the right.'

Mr Evans turned out to be tall slim man in a beautifully tailored uniform, just the right amount of white shirt cuff showing with plain gold links gleaming in the lamp light. He turned a grey, weary face with bloodshot brown eyes toward me, 'what is it son?'

I handed over my discharge book with the company orders tucked inside. The chief read them slowly. 'You will find that we run a different ship aboard the M.V. *Plymouth,* compared to the others I observe in your book, however the shore side superintendent must think you are up for it. Our skipper is ex-Royal Navy and still on reserve, he's a stickler for 'spit and polish', and Commodore of our large fleet to boot. We carry a limited number of passengers in some style, I might add, but basically our business is cargo. Outward bound it's mostly manufactured goods, but on the return voyage it's frozen food. Meat, apples and such like and for that reason we carry an extra compliment of refrigeration engineers. I tell you this because our catering staff is considerably larger than one would normally expect.'

He picked up a phone and called someone called Jack to come in. 'Jack is my second in command; he'll show you to your berth, report back here in an hour when you've settled in.'

'Yes sir,' I replied wondering at the beautiful timber panelling and brass work. I turned to see Jack the second standing in the cabin entry uniformed in a similar fashion as the chief, I held out my hand to shake, 'Hi, Tom Morgan captain's steward'

Jack had a world-weary air; he ignored the offered hand, 'Follow me Morgan.'

We set off down the customary alleyway painted in fresh gleaming white. To my delight the cabin I was shown into was a single berth with a tiny en suite bathroom. 'Wow! Is this all mine?' All the bed linen and towels were on the timber sided bunk, every article emblazoned with the company logo. Two spacious drawers sat beneath the bunk and an adequate wardrobe sat beside a writing table with a lamp on gimbals. A leather settee was fitted beneath the porthole.

'We all have single berth accommodation Morgan; this is 1959 you know, I don't know what other scows you've sailed in but this shipping company is the best, and we expect the best from our crew.'

I stared at the prim little mouth in a pasty face crowned by carefully combed black hair,

'I don't think I'm going to get on with you mate,' I thought as he glanced down at his watch, 'the chief said you are required to turn to, in one hour, here are your company epaulettes and uniform buttons; make sure they are on your white mess jacket when you do.' The shining silver buttons with the company flag embossed upon them were held in place through eyelets in the jacket by a small pin. The smart crimson and blue braided epaulettes fastened the same way.

However right at this moment, I felt in urgent need of a cup of tea after the long journey across the city. Hastily unpacking, and before changing, I went to the galley situated amidships. Stepping over the stormwater coaming onto the damp galley deck, it had just been washed down; I saw before me the back of a huge figure of a man. The broad shoulders clad in a straining white tee shirt tapered down to narrow hips encased in a cooks checked work trousers.

'Oh no!' I exclaimed, 'I'd know that head anywhere.'

The big man turned slowly, 'Who the heck are you?'

'What, you don't remember me?'

'Why the hell should I?'

The once athletic figure had developed a paunch. 'Looks like you've been eating too much of your own grub William.' I grinned.

'Piss off out of my galley you twit.'

'You really don't remember me do you? You were at the *Vindicatrix* training ship, with me in 1955.' The cook's rugged face peered closer; Billy Pitt had one green eye and one blue. The nose had suffered too many punches, but the generous mouth split into a huge dimple cheeked grin. 'My goodness! It that the posh cocky git from Surrey?'

'You'd better believe it Billy boy, any chance of a cuppa I'm parched?'

He grabbed my hand in a vice like grip and pumped it up and down.

'What are you doing here, and what happened to the nose, slowing up are you?'

'I'm the new captain's steward so you had better be nice.'

'Bulls***! You, the last time we met you couldn't get out of your way.'

'Now then Bill be nice, we're going on a long voyage together be a pal and brew me a strong cup of tea.'

The big man lumbered over to a copper urn and poured hot water on a handful of tea leaves and set the silver pot on the stove to brew. I marvelled at the strange coincidence that brought us together again. My hometown in the south, and the east-end origins of Billy Pitt could not have been further apart; the thought of sailing with him gave me immense pleasure. William 'Billy' Pitt had been at the end of his training when we met; he had trialled for West Ham Football club and had rowed for his riverside club on 'The Isle of Dogs.'

As he poured the tea, I remarked,

'I'd never have taken you for a cook mate.'

'Better than being a ruddy steward, I tried it with P & O but couldn't stand the bulls*** and switched to the galley and its second cook, my chief is not all that fond of stewards either' he grinned.

Thereafter it started all over again, the camaraderie, the friendly rivalry and all the things that turn men into good friends. I, to Bill's amusement, regaled him with the voyage and consequences of the not so good ship *Barranca*, including the nose job, Trinidad, and sundry females. As I was about to leave for the chief's office he said in a very stern tone,

'By the way Morg a couple of rules to be going on with, don't come down off the bridge with special requests from his highness he gets the same to eat as the rest of the officers.'

'Turned into a "red rag" socialist have we? I'll tell him that when he entertains dignitaries in foreign ports.'

'That's different; we all get a bit extra then. Most of us have been aboard since the "maiden" voyage. She's a good ship, fast and stable and the grub is tops. All the deck hands are from the islands off the coast of Scotland, darn good seamen and keep very much to themselves. The engine room blokes are a pretty good lot, except for the engineers, why is it they are always a pain in the arse? The chief cook is great, lets the rest of us get on with it most of the time "Elegant" Evans, our chief and Purser is all right, but watch that slimy second steward, if ever a man should have stayed ashore and become a penny-pinching clerk it's "Black Jack". Then of course we've got "Languid Lily" acting "Tiger", but really only a half decent waitress in the saloon.'

'Well I'd better get on with it I'll see you later and we can catch up.'

Mr Evans was waiting impatiently. 'Ah Morgan, all kitted out I see. Introductions I think, skipper first.'

Evans led the way up three decks; on the way I observed timber panelled bulkheads and portraits of various dignitaries and one of a youthful Queen Elizabeth. The top deck companion way had a polished timber rail and carpet on the treads. This is a very long way from *Barranca*, first impression close to luxury.

The chief steward knocked quietly on a burled walnut cabin door.

'Enter,' came a well modulated order, 'ah chief, so this is my new man, welcome aboard young fella, your shore side chappie tells me you were at the Savoy and have actually served the Queen and Prince Phillip at the Hyde Park, well done, good show, judging from the size of you, lifeboat drill will be a piece of cake!' These drills are carried out at least twice whilst in port and my place would be with the skipper. 'Thank you sir,' I replied.

Glancing around me I noticed a quantity of small china ornaments set out on a fake mantelpiece that surrounded of all things a fake log fire. I wondered what would happen to them at sea when the weather got a bit frisky.

'I won't need you for the rest of today, Mr Evans will fill you in on your duties and Morgan my morning tea will be served punctually at 0600. That's all for now.'

It turned out that Captain Nielsen had a great many foibles, one of which was that his uniform be pressed daily, his washing done twice a week and the miniature china creatures from Beatrix Potter's world be wrapped in cotton wool and stored carefully in a box once the ship sailed.

Nielsen was a big man, an inch or two taller than me, however he had a portly bearing and with his balding hairline and penchant for the good life, I christened him Mr Pickwick in my mind. His numerous uniforms and suits all tailored in Savile Row hung in a special storeroom, he ordered shirts by the dozen from Italy and they were made from fine Swiss cotton. I was to learn he treated the entire crew with respect, his voice civil even in reprimand. Apart from taking care of the captain's cabin my other duties, very pleasant in fact, were to take charge of the small bar in the lounge when our eight passengers came aboard. Captain Nielsen drank one pink gin before lunch and another before dinner and taught me the way he liked it made, I also served the meals at the Captain's table.

Five days after I joined her, busy days of storing at a frenzied rate the *Plymouth* was ready to sail. No wonder the chief steward looked frazzled; he was the pivot of almost all the activity for the comfort of passengers and crew. For some crewmembers, it is an exciting moment, for others sad and for men like me a relief to be under way again. The passengers came aboard and then under the guidance of the river pilot the graceful ship slipped slowly down to Sheerness where the pilot left us. All four staterooms were full for the voyage to New Zealand. All the minutiae of a well-drilled catering department fell into place. Robbie, the bedroom steward and I carried the baggage to the allotted cabins ignoring the fuss and chatter all around us as best we could. Robert Arnold was an old hand; with calm precision he guided the four fluttering women and their trying-oh-so-hard to be world-weary traveller husbands, together with the right cabin baggage to the correct berth. As he deposited the people he would pamper for the next four weeks he quietly assured them that dinner would be served at seven o' clock, no need to dress first night out, and the bar opened at six.

'My name is Rob and this is Tom the captain's steward. Tom will serve you in the bar and have the captains seating plan ready when you come down, if I can be of service this afternoon just ring the bell which is situated above your writing desk.'

Robbie, a quiet little man, in his late fifties rotund and balding wore the shiniest black shoes I had ever seen, they encased flat feet that turned out when he walked, these feet often the butt of jibes from a curly haired steward in his early twenties, who, like me hailed from south London.

This ever smiling fellow looked after the chief engineer and helped me out in the bar at night, his name was Ron. Robbie explained with a theatrical sigh that the feet were the result of, 'To many years on the "*Queen Mary*," you should see the length of those alleyways.'

"Languid Lilly" was a sight to behold, tall and skinny as a rake with rounded shoulders and a long pale face surmounted by a thatch of unruly yellow hair, he had a lazy way of moving. Real name Lionel he treated me with total distain. As officers' steward he cleaned their cabins and made up the bunks of all four deck officers, the two cadets whom shared a two berth, and also that of the chief steward, a lot of work and a come down from captain's steward.

The other engineer's steward Ronnie Wilson, came from Birmingham, and spoke with the distinctive dialect of the area. With dark good looks, tight curly hair with a short and sturdy build he had a great sense of humour, that kept all of us in a state of hilarity during service, much to "Black Jack's" disapproval.

Each of the stewards had a table of six to serve at meal times, the officers and passengers mixed together. Watch officers took their meals when relieved of duty. The seating arrangements for twenty eight officers and passengers were rarely filled, except at Commodore Nielsen's table. The chief engineer presided over one of the other four round tables, as did the first mate; the fourth belonged to 'Elegant' Evans who much preferred a tray in his office due to the infernal complaints about trivial matters.

Billy Pitt had introduced me to the rest of his lads in the galley. One a singing baker from Liverpool by name Jimmy, a merry fellow who knew all the folk songs and dirty ditties which he sang in a melodious voice which emanated from a crooked mouth set beneath a huge nose; in fact a face only a mother could love. His bread cakes and deserts a marvel. Jimmy and Barney never let up on one another during service giving much amusement to the others.

Kevin the butcher, also from Liverpool, was a sophisticated man with a taste for Baroque music; he also enjoyed Traditional jazz and was to introduce me to his collection of New Orleans music. We often got together after work to listen to Kevin's portable record player and enjoy the two cans of beer we were allowed to buy from the 'slops chest' each day. Chris Barber our favourite British band shared equal billing with the Dutch Swing College and many of the New Orleans greats helped pass the long nights as we crossed the oceans to the other side of the world.

Strangely enough, compared with the old *Barranca*, the various divisions of the crew mingled more due to the fact that each department had a mess where they could relax and we often challenged one another at darts. As *Plymouth* cruised slowly down to the Azores the skipper drilled the men in lifeboat and emergency procedures and inspected the ship from stem to stern every Wednesday and Sunday. For those who wished to attend a religious service he conducted one, C of E, in the passenger lounge at ten on Sunday morning.

All of this came as a refreshing lift to my career. I rejoiced in the efficiency of a smooth running modern turbine driven vessel. All of which was about to change as we cruised across the Atlantic heading for Panama. At 0200, shortly after we sailed from the Azores all the emergency bells and sirens went off in a great clangour of sound.

Staggering from my bunk, I pulled on some clothes and ran like a hare to my station beside a stormwater door aft of the passenger accommodation. The Captain's voice as calm and precise as always came over the Tannoy speaker system.

'This is not a drill, I repeat not a drill, all passengers will go to their lifeboat stations, please wear your lifejackets and warm clothing.'

Most of the passengers milled around flapping their arms and yelling for an explanation. Robbie passed quietly amongst them making sure they had their lifejackets on. Just then Captain Nielsen's precise voice came over the Tannoy again.

'We have a fire in the engine room. I beg all of you to keep calm. Members of the crew stay at your emergency stations and do nothing without specific orders. Our engineers are dealing with the situation.'

Standing by the watertight door that I had to close on the given order, I tried to visualise the scene down below. Men in grimy white overalls carrying fire extinguishers filled with the chemicals required to quell oily electrical flare-ups, dashing the stuff on the flames and praying to their gods for salvation. The last place I would want to be is down in the bowels of a ship in distress.

'All crew will execute their emergency orders and report to your lifeboat station on the double.'

I wound the lever that closed the heavy steel door and ran to the boat deck. We had four lifeboats each with a petrol engine, they also had a mast and sail that could be stepped and used if required, plus six oars. Each boat had a crew comprising a deck officer, an engineer, some deck hands and the rest of us scattered evenly amongst them. The order came to swing out the boats to the end of the davits; we waited calmly for the order to lower away.

The officer in charge a nervous young fourth mate tense with the moment as indeed we all were. 'Excuse me sir, shall we get the covers off her?'

In the flurry the young officer had neglected this obvious part of the drill. The question came from an elderly seaman, who by the look of him had a great deal of experience in such matters. Realising his error in the tension of the moment, the young officer snapped a brusque, 'Very good McLeod, please do so.'

'It'd help a lot if we have to scarper,' the old chap said quietly to me.

I gazed around at the sea and the sky, fortunately both were calm, a soft warm breeze moved the air around all four lifeboats as they hung a short step from the ship's side. Crew and passengers waited stoically ready to jump the moment the order came. One man, a passenger clutching a fat brief case, already seated in one of the boats refused to come out on the first mate's command, an elderly lady passenger comforted a young woman with gentle pats on her arm; otherwise all seemed calm.

In the eerie silence, broken only by the swish of water on the ships hull and a vibration from the emergency generators, every murmur, every cough, the scraping of a shoe on the teak deck, was magnified as if by a giant microphone in the sky.

The captain's voice cracking with relief cried through the Tannoy, 'Stand down, I repeat stand down, hoist in the lifeboats, all passengers report to the lounge. Crew members report to your officers. All is under control. I repeat stand down.'

By the time I arrived in the galley, the 'scuttlebutt' had all the information.

'Back to the Azores,' Billy told me, 'most of the electrical systems are shot.' Thank the Lord we are only three days out of the Azores, I'd hate to be closer to Panama and have to put into one the Caribbean islands for repairs.

'What will they do with the passengers?' This whispered enquiry came from one of the stewards' boys.

'Why we'll boil 'em in oil and feed 'em to the sharks for bringing bad luck to as fine a body of men as ever set foot on a ship's deck,' this of course came from Jimmy the incorrigible baker, who burst into the first chorus of an old sea shanty.

"FIFTEEN MEN ON A DEAD MAN'S CHEST

YO HO HO AND A BOTTLE OF RUM."

'Rum my arse,' cried Bill,' you'll get beer and like it.' This helped to dispel the tension and Billy pulled a dozen cans of pale ale out of the cool room and shared them around. The mood among the men decidedly relieved, the thought of many hours in an open boat had not appealed.

Next morning, as the ship limped along on one engine with the lighting down by half, and that only shakily provided by an emergency generator, conversation centred upon the result of this unforseen episode. Frantic messages flew from the radio room, mainly to the boardroom of the shipping company, but also from panicked passengers. Ultimately the decisions would be made in Leadenhall Street: the economics of repairs, what to do with the passengers and crew, who goes who stays, many a rumour circulated, none of which could be given any credibility.

At six o'clock that evening, the chief engineer's estimate of damage had been digested and discussed back at head office. M.V. *Plymouth* would deposit her passengers at company expense in a hotel in Tenerife, thence to be conveyed back to London by plane. The fire had been caused by a malfunction in one of the modules controlling the computer that virtually ran the engines. Swan and Edgars would send an engineer and a computer "Whiz kid" to analyse the damage and order the equipment to fix it, the expected delay three weeks.

Captain Nielsen had by this time decided that he and I suited one another admirably. When a skeleton crew of volunteers was called for to remain aboard, the Commodore made sure I was one of them. I had no desire to return home anyway. About one fifth of the crew remained aboard, including Billy Pitt and Jimmy the baker to feed us. The rest were paid off and flown home.

On most evenings in this tropical haven, Bill and I strolled down to the local pub and had a pint or two after work. Jimmy who was married with a couple of children only came down on Saturday nights when an amateur trio played in a corner to entertain the locals. On one such Saturday Jimmy announced that today was his birthday. After a couple of weeks of regular evening pints, we had become well known to the customers at 'The Red Bull', a tourist trap made up to look like an English pub. The little band struck up an out of key version of "Happy Birthday," and Jimmy gave out with a rendition with a few ripe choruses added, which the crowded bar lapped up. His melodious voice thrilled the audience and he had to give them more. Eventually he urged Billy and me up with him and we gave forth with *Barefoot Days* with lyrics that the author would never have dreamed of.

Three weeks and four days later with all ship shape again, most of the crew after an unexpected leave drifted back aboard. Languid Lilly was the only absentee from the catering list; she was replaced by a sombre Swede. I was well pleased to see Ronnie the engineer's steward return. Robbie fussed over the state of the accommodation on the passenger deck, and had it all gleaming by the time our new group arrived from London. Amongst them on this cruise, we were to carry some VIPs. One of them was the widow of a whisky magnate and the other an apple baron from Tasmania; according to instructions from Leadenhall Street they would need special attention. As usual, Robbie had them settled and eating out of his hand in no time.

The Australian apple grower Archie Jones and his wife Millie, also had a factory that made jams and preserves a quality product that apparently sold all around the world, they were the salt of the earth; however the whisky dowager was another kind of human being all together. Mrs McClure became the butt of below deck humour, most of it black. Nothing was ever quite right, the pernickety old witch found fault in everything from Commodore Nielsen's daily lottery to guess the number of nautical miles the ship had travelled in twenty four hours, the tiresome safety drills, the 1100 hours beef tea never strong enough, Jimmy's scones, bread and cakes, nowhere as good as her own. The meals she ate would choke a horse but the sauces gravies or the vegetables never quite right. An angular woman with iron-grey hair and a piecing blue eye, she sat at the skipper's right hand, tapping her diamond-laden fingers and passing acidic comments on all and sundry.

On one particular evening the sole Bonne Femme was not to her liking. The sauce, made with a delicate white wine and slivers of mushroom, far too overpowering she claimed, to which Millie Jones sitting on the captains left remarked, 'On the contrary,' and gesturing to me she said, 'Thomas please give my compliments to Mr Pitt, the sauce is perfect.'

Everyone noted the heavy emphasis on the Mister. Once out in the galley serving area I relayed the episode embroidering the skipper's choked expression.

'I thought the 'old man' was about to burst a boiler, he'll never last all trip without giving the old biddy what for.'

It actually happened two days later; the widow remarked at the pre luncheon drinks that two Labrador dogs we were conveying in specially built pens, did not get enough exercise. Captain Neilson placed his pink gin carefully on the bar and turning his sea-bronzed countenance toward her he announced loud enough for all to hear, 'Ah my Lady, you are a dog lover amongst all your other attributes, may I suggest you relieve my lamp trimmer of the task, you would no doubt benefit from the walking yourself.'

'What are you inferring Captain?'

'Only that a daily constitutional benefits one and all your Ladyship.'

Behind the bar I turned my attention to slicing lemon for the gin and tonics, carefully removing all the pips, when I looked up I thought perhaps her Ladyship had swallowed one.

'Captain; May I remind you that my late husband was a director of this company and we supply your vessels with excellent whisky at a very advantageous price?'

'Ah there again I must question your information madam. To the best of my knowledge your late departed husband was a director twice removed; a small holding group in which he had shares, a conglomerate so to speak held the shares in question.'

Turning to me, he asked, 'Thomas which whisky would you estimate is the most popular on this ship?'

'Well we go through a lot of Haig and Teachers sir.'

'And her Ladyship's brand?'

'We've had a case aboard since I joined sir, there's a bottle right up there on the optic with a couple of drams gone, and to my knowledge the carton has several bottles still remaining.'

The others present held their collective breath.

'Well really,' her face a chalky white, the grinding of teeth almost audible, her Ladyship swept from the elegant cocktail bar.

After that she spent a great deal more time in her stateroom. The atmosphere aboard altered for the good as *Plymouth* retraced the nautical miles of my earlier voyages, this time in altogether different circumstances across the wide reaches of the mid Atlantic. The weather was most favourable; we had warm sunny days and cool nights, as we cruised into the Caribbean Sea. Without stopping to savour any of the delights offered by these scattered islands we arrived in Colon at the start of the Panama Canal. Those aboard who had never traversed this engineering marvel stood at the rails and watched as the great ship of 7000 tons was smoothly conveyed through lock after lock into the Pacific Ocean at Panama City. For the convenience of the passengers we stayed alongside the wharf for the rest of the day and night. Some went ashore to see the sights, others who knew that there was nothing to see, stayed aboard.

Our new course took us just north of the Galapagos Islands close enough for the passengers to view the group of mysterious atolls through binoculars then set a direct course for Pitcairn Island in the South Pacific. The smooth progress so far recorded erupted into violent squalls accompanied by downpours of rain that hit the deck like 'stair rods' as the pantry boy quaintly put it. Ferocious winds tore across the vast expanse of the Pacific with nothing to hinder their progress. Waves as high as office blocks thundered down in mighty crashes causing the *Plymouth* to shudder and shake, dip and dive, and stagger onward. Even the hardiest members of the crew were appalled and numbed into a dazed robot like attention to their duties. All the passengers were sick and stayed in their bunks, the safest place, with the decks bucking and weaving and streaming with water.

Cooking meals in these conditions became a nightmare. The surface of the stove was braced up with heavy stainless steel bars slotted into brackets that held the pans in place. Each pot filled to about half the usual content to stop it slopping over the side.

In this kind of extreme weather all the tables and the sideboard in the saloon are covered with a double layer of wet linen tablecloths to stop cruets, cutlery and glassware from sliding about and rails attached to the table edges on hinges are raised in order to stop plates of food, or even the food itself slopping into the laps of the diners.

The bosun strung ropes made of light heaving line everywhere there was a space that might be dangerous to cross in safety without aid, and that included the galley. Many a slip and fall was saved by this precaution. For thirty-six hours the elements raged. Inside the ship the air grew stale and heavy with moisture; the air conditioning had given up and an alarming vibration added to the chief engineer's problems. The shafts that drove the twin propellers, housed in a covered channel from the engine room to the stern, began to over heat.

During all this Robbie cleaned up vomit from cabin floors, and attended to his charges like a well trained nurse. He cared for them with good humour and little homilies, together with lots of dry toast. Robert Arnold knew his ministrations would result in cash being slipped gratefully into his ready hand practically doubling his monthly salary at the end of the voyage; what's more it would be tax free. If he were a good fellow he would share a proportion with the cooks a case of beer and a bottle of rum.

In the early evening of the second day of the deluge Mr Dalrymple, the chief engineer, a tall thin stick of a man with a prominent Adam's apple, and thinning red hair rang the bridge.

The officer of the watch picked up the instrument, 'Bridge,' he answered nervously as another towering wave caused the ship to dive beneath thundering foam.

'I need the skipper urgently Mike.'

'That's easy chief he's right here.'

Nielsen sat strapped into the pilot's chair staring morosely at the barometer and listening to the weather reports from the Hawaii Coast Guard.

'What is it Chief?'

'Captain every time we pitch into a wave the screws come out of the sea and with no water to thrust against they spin like crazy, this is causing a dramatic increase in revs and the heat in the tunnel is way up and this in turn is creating the shuddering you hear through the hull.'

'We have to keep her head on into the seas Keith otherwise we'll surely broach.'

'I understand Skip, can I slow the revs down?'

'Ease them down chief until I tell you to stop, we have to keep a certain amount of headway on her ok?' The chief's Glaswegian voice snarled, 'Aye captain.'

For three more days and nights we laboured onward until the blessed golden sun raised its beaming face. The heavy seas had taken their toll on the twin propellers and drive shafts as a result our speed was now half our normal rate of a steady seventeen knots. As a result we made a stop in Pitcairn Island for fresh fruit and veg, it was rowed out in very large boats which on the Thames would be called wherries. Clouds shrouded most of the island from view. I would have dearly loved to go ashore and meet the descendents of the *Bounty Mutiny*.

We arrived in Auckland several days late, and whilst the engineers got on with repairs to bearings and seals, Commodore Nielsen got on with PR. Which meant yours truly had to be on the ball and the galley staff busy preparing snacks and nibbles on sticks. My mate Ron was to assist behind the bar.

Shipping agents, stevedore bosses, customs officials, immigration free loaders all came aboard with awe struck girls from the typing pool. Ron, a bit of a lad with the girls eyed off a tasty brunette and gave her a bit of the old patter.

Much later in the proceedings, a petite, beautifully dressed woman of middle years came quietly into the room. Nielsen's face lit up like that of a schoolboy. Dressed in the fashion of the time in a smart navy two piece suit, she wore a small white hat and white gloves with white shoes and handbag. Her face unadorned by make-up, shone with good health.

'Elise, how good of you to come,' his smile spoke volumes.

'Phillip, at last you are here, I had quite given you up to storm and tempest.'

Introductions followed, and taking her elbow Nielsen steered her over to the bar. 'May I have Teachers whiskey and water no ice please? Her eyes, hazel in colour, soft and bright at the same time, brushed lightly over me with very little warmth in them.

'This is my steward Tom, anything you want just ask, Tom this is Lady McIntyre, her husband is down in Antarctica doing great things.'

'I bet you'll be doing great things yourself tonight Phillip dear,' I thought as I smiled quietly to myself.

The bums and stiffs as Ron called them left the ship around 7:30pm. At this time, the officers, those not on duty at the bar, had finished their evening meal and Billy Pitt had put up a cold buffet for those remaining. Some were going ashore as guests of the VIPs. In the now empty lounge, Ron and I joined by Billy Pitt downed a couple, courtesy of the shipping company and adjourned to their mess. Black Jack our erstwhile second steward whilst sniffing suspiciously at the whisky fumes in the air informed us that,

'The chief is drawing up a roster, so that while we are on the coast the catering crew can have an afternoon off once a week. You of course Mister Morgan will be on call at the Captain's whim, other than that as we have no passengers, after lunch daily you are free as a bird.' Bill peered in mock seriousness at me,

'You do realise of course that these barbarian Kiwis close their pubs at 6 o' clock, don't you?'

'Ah well, it behoves us to get an early start then does it not Mister Pitt.'

'If you say so me old china,' he accepted with grin.

After a game or two of darts and a hand of gin rummy, all the lads were turned in with a cup of cocoa warming their slumbers. With the exception of those who knew where to go for a "sly grog", illegal after hours drinking.

The next day dawned much like the first, heavy grey cloud above and a steady chilly wind from the south. I wondered if the Duke, or Lord McIntyre or whatever he was, had taken warm clothes to keep him as snug as her Ladyship was that morning. The Commodore's bunk had not been slept in.

At 1500 hours on the dot Messer's Pitt and Morgan dressed in their casual best, bounced down the gangway. With a cheery "don't wait up" to the watchman we were gone.

We wandered as tourists do; rode on the funicular rail car, admired the heavy Victorian architecture, stood at the ferry terminal, the sea link between North and South Islands, and watched a large green ferry dock fighting a nasty wind.

At around 1700 hours it was definitely time for a beer, we adjourned to the Post Office Hotel. Whoever had modelled this bar and all the others we would encounter, must have been scholars in the same school of bad taste. It was a place in which to do nothing but drink alcohol, a few touches of Victorian elegance still survived, but the overall effect was drink up and be gone. At ten minutes before closing time the friendly barman leaned conspiratorially toward and with a wink said,

'If you lads need another drink pop up those stairs over there, order a plate of food and you can stay all night if you want.'

'Well done old son,' Billy exclaimed. On the bar several coins of the realm sat scattered in a pool of beer, 'keep that lot for services rendered matey.'

At the top of the staircase the décor changed for the better. The theme was of pseudo French provincial, green and gold wallpapers added a classy mood and velvet drapes adorned the high Victorian windows which together with cream tables and chairs scattered on a field of deep green carpet that sported a delicate cream fleur-de-lis motif was at once relaxing and inviting.

'This is more like it,' I grinned, 'I'm not used to slumming it you know.'

'Bulls*** Morgan! You would drink alcohol from tinkers jockstrap if that was all there was.'

'Now you are being nasty Bill, if you don't simmer down I shall tell those young ladies behind the bar that you've had quite enough and should be ejected.'

'Would you look at that,' chuckled Bill as he advanced at a trot to the counter.

'Are you two gentlemen staying in the hotel?' The tiny blonde one asked with a dimpled smile. 'Not unless that is an invitation, Bill replied, 'we require nothing more than a drink and a meal if that is all right with you darling?'

'Cheek, I'm not your darling, you must be off one of the ships in port.'

'Now how did you guess that? My mate and I are here on special assignment, carrying the Commodore of the fleet to far flung parts of the Empire. I'm Bill and this is Tommy the Tiger, you'd best watch out for him. Two beers and the menu there's a love.'

Seated at the end of the bar two old gents glared, one of them gave a loud grunt; turning to his drinking partner, he proclaimed in a voice that carried to Bill and I,

'Cheeky young bastards, a bit of time in the army would do them a bit of good.'

Squeezing Bills arm gently to stop his outcry, I turned a heavy unblinking gaze on the old gentlemen.

'Now then gents, I can see by your lapel badges that you have done your bit for the Empire, and more power to you, however if you think Korea is just the Queens tea party, I'll soon put you right on that.'

The man who had not spoken coloured up and said, 'Sorry young fella me mate gets carried away after a few, and he don't mean no harm.' My dear old Mother had tried hard to have me speak English in a proper manner and now my officer accent had taken over and my persona had changed.

'Not at all, would you care to have drink? we are on a goodwill tour you know from the 'old dart', the Commodore gave us specific instructions to be courteous at all times to the natives.'

By this time, Billy Pitt was near to bursting. The two bar maids fighting to control their giggles. 'What ever they require,' I ordered with a flourish of the hand, 'and one for yourselves, I think the goulash will do very nicely, what say you William?'

'Jolly good old sport, do they have wine here do you think?'

'That's enough Bill, beer will do fine.' I murmured as taking him by the shoulder I steered a course for a corner table.

'You b***** posh Surrey gits can't half bung it on when you want.'

During the very ordinary meal, eye contact between the girls led to a muffled consultation regarding the time they got off duty. 'Well ten o' clock really, but as you two are the only customers left when you're ready. Look boys, you can't get a drink in this town at this hour, why don't we grab a couple of bottles and go up to our room?'

Hardly containing our joy we paid the bill, grabbed the bottles and stumbled up the darkened stairs to the servant's quarters. The dark haired Vikki led the way with a promising sway to her rump and the diminutive blonde Chrissie brought up the rear with many a whispered, 'Quiet you lot, you'll wake the whole b***** pub.'

Next morning, in a weak sunshine, Bill and I stumbled back to the *Plymouth.* 'What a night' we both chortled on our way down the dock

'It was seeing those old codgers off that did it you know; those poor kids had been putting up with their bulls*** night after night for months on end.'

'Yeah, but I think your toffee nosed officer accent reminded them of past glories, I thought you were going to tell them you were with the Gloucester Regiment on that b***** hill where they ran out of ammo.'

'Definitely not, old fruit,' I remonstrated, 'there are times when to say less, is more, if you get my drift.'

Once on board we headed for the showers; arriving in the galley we received a "Bronx" cheer from the rest of the lads. 'And where do you two think you've been, Mother waited up half the night?' This query, in a put on arch female voice came from Jimmy the baker. Of course Ron had to chip in with,

'Daddy would spank if he didn't think you'd enjoy it.'

'Get to work you lot, or I'll be doing the b***** spanking on the bridge,' growled Billy, still working off a sizable hangover.

The rest of the week passed with Bill and me, with the addition of Ronnie, who insisted on being in on the action, at the hotel as often as possible. At the very top of the old building, in what had once been accommodation for servants, all the staff, which included chamber maids, bar tenders, hall porters, receptionists and sundry others who lived-in, had rooms opening onto one long corridor. The doors never seemed to stop opening and closing at night. Ron with his sharp wit christened it the "street of twisted faces."

On the night before the *Plymouth* sailed for the South Island, "the street," gave a party. By midnight the noise became uproar as Vikki began a strip routine. The ultimate item of clothing never came off as the senior manager banged noisily on the door and threatened to sack the lot of them: the three seamen were threatened with the "full force of the law", unless they departed forthwith never ever to return.

'Forthwith!' echoed Ron as we tumbled down four flights of stairs, rushing into the street and heading for the adjacent dockside.

In the late 50s maritime trade was crucial to the Commonwealth; sheep for meat and fleece, fruit, wheat, beef and cattle hides, were exchanged for machinery, luxury goods, cars, diesel trains, finished fabrics, and so the docks, a vital link in the freight system were established much closer to city transport links. Everyone in NZ must have been very honest because there were no dock walls or gates.

A short walk and we straggled up the gangway. Mercifully the night watchman was occupied elsewhere. Scrawled on a small blackboard at the gangway head, the legend, "Sailing at 0500", greeted our bloodshot eyes.

'Blimey! It's a b***** good job that bloke threw us out, we may have missed her else.'

Thankfully, I sank onto my bunk knowing the watch would wake me on time to see to the skipper's needs.

Twenty-four hours or so later, I leaned on the starboard rail gazing at the horizon. A mug of strong early morning tea steamed in my fist; the breaking day offered a low cumulus cloud cover over a sea of gunmetal grey. A purple mountain range broke the shoreline. Soft shades of pink and mauve softly stroked the underbelly of the heavy clouds as the sun rose. A whale, no more than a fleeting obsidian flash surfaced, and with a gracefully arched back, spouted, and sank beneath the waves. It was at that moment that I fell in love with this magnificent country. New Zealand was new, unspoiled by "Old World" prejudice; there was room to move and to start anew. Bluff, a small fishing town at the southern tip of the South Island, was cold when we arrived, blustery winds from the Antarctic buffeted sea birds on high. We sat in solitude in an empty café and ate what appeared to be the national fare, steak and eggs. After discharging cargo, we turned northward again, first Lyttelton, then Napier, and with holds empty headed back to Wellington. Discretion urged us to phone the girls to see if the coast was clear.

'Don't you dare set foot in this place, old misery will have your guts for garters, and we will see you at the Orient about four.' At the Orient calamity struck: Vikki reckoned she was having Billy's baby.

'Oh yeah, and my old mum is St Theresa,' he exploded with venom, 'we've only been gone two weeks, you silly cow, go get the real "geezer." Come on Tom let's get the hell out of this rat trap.' A screaming match ensued, which had us out on the street in no time. Loading was over in five days, during which time neither Pitt nor I ventured ashore and refused to accept 'phone calls.

The picturesque town of New Plymouth on the west coast was the next loading point. This small community is nestled on the edge of Egmont National Park. The park took its name from a picture book mountain with a snow-covered peak that lay a few miles to the east. The air was clean and crisp, and the sea sparkled with dancing light. The natural deep water provided safe mooring for large ships.

The day after *Plymouth* berthed, one of Shaw Savills fleet, a huge passenger liner called the *Dominion Monarch* sailed in flying the long red pennant of a ship on its final voyage. Over the years, this ship had picked up a reputation for signing on the 'riff raff' of the Merchant Marine as crew. The crew's facilities so bad, that only the most desperate of men looking for work signed on. It was rumoured that on one particular voyage, a diesel locomotive being carried as deck cargo, was deliberately loosened by a disgruntled crewmember from its securing cables, and tossed over the side into a lively sea, carrying away a goodly portion of the side rail and causing untold damage.

That reputation was confirmed on Saturday night at a local dance. Despite dire warnings from parents, the bored teenagers of this one horse town came in their usual numbers to 'rock' to the latest hit records from Elvis, Fats Domino, Chuck Berry, and 'smooch' to 'The Platters' and Sam Cooke. At the dance, the crew's off these ships stood out like fiery beacons due to the clothes they wore. The *Teddy Boy,* dress craze was effected by some of the Brits off this ship: long four button jackets with velvet collars and 'stove pipe' trousers; others influenced by American music came in blue jeans, some like Bill and I in smartly tailored suits, we all searched for dancing partners in the clamour.

The girls were out numbered ten to one, and it did not take long for inter ship rivalry to surface. Somebody from the "DM" clobbered a local, a deckhand from the *Plymouth* clobbered him and it was on for all hands. Bill and I retreated to a handy corner and waited.

'Always have a wall, or preferably a corner at your back in times of trouble, Thomas my son, wait 'til they get off the first flurry of harmless punches, and the fire in their belly is cooling and then attack.'

Order began to be restored, but one battle scarred little man with a heavy Scots accent stood in the middle of the dance floor yelling, 'Come on then you pussies see these fists, they are made for belting Sassenachs.' The rest of his gang stood menacingly on the edge of the polished surface. That was enough for Bill.

'Enough is enough you little gob s****, leave these people alone and get back to that b***** menace to shipping and take your stupid mates with you.'

'Oh boy Billy, now you've done it.'

Sure enough, an ominous silence lasting about three seconds ensued. The Scot turned his eyes to our corner. He saw two big men taking off their jackets; both had noses that had seen better days. The bigger of the two glared out of eyes of a different hue. Three or four men of our crew shuffled up to take a stance beside them.

'Well now if it's not the pretty boys off that little scow next to us lads.'

The line of six *Plymouth* pretty boys advanced as one, the so-called 'hard men' of the "DM" disappeared like smoke. 'It always amazes me,' Pitt chortled turning to his relieved companions, 'bullies are all piss and wind, the buggers always go to water under a concerted attack. Well done lads, extra portions of plum duff all round tomorrow.'

The ancient liner, heading for the scrap yard, sailed the next day. The long pennant drooped sadly at her masthead, our galley boy, on a trip to the vegetable locker, (a wooden cage on the upper deck), disturbed by the previous night's ruckus, and the mournful note of the departing ship's foghorn salute, threw a rotten potato at the departing vessel, a very sad ending to the ship's illustrious career.

The Maori names of the seaports, villages, and towns fascinated me, Wanganui, Taranaki, Otaki, and the tongue twister Paekakariki. Of the major ports, mostly named after their European founders, Llyttelton came next, the gateway to, or the departure point for most of the South Island's produce.

Christchurch, the major city of the South Island, lay within a short train ride of the docks. On the two-carriage train, travelling on my own to investigate that city, I observed rolling green countryside. With time to myself, because of the skipper's absence, I wandered around the streets of what seemed to be the replica of a large English town of many churches that had been lifted bodily from the green fields and country lanes of Kent or Sussex, and then placed gently beside a river in this magical setting.

Returning late in the afternoon, I decided on a cold beer. Why I chose that particular hotel in the main street is the way that fate traps us poor humans. Seated at the bar was Ron, and beside him an enormous Maori woman overflowing the barstool.

'Hi-ya Morg, meet Mona, we're waiting for the rest of the gang, pull up a stool and have a beer. Mona this Tom Morgan.'

Expecting a deep rumble of a voice from the vast chest of the woman, I was surprised by the soft tones and a gentle handshake. Mona had the flat features of her race, which lit up in a beautiful white-toothed smile; a gold incisor slightly marred the genuine warmth of a friendly greeting.

Three beers arrived and the barman said, with a nod, 'They are here.'

Turning toward the door I saw two Maori men and three women approaching across the room. The tallest of the men was a great ugly brute with tattoos all over his face and arms, the other short and wide of shoulder, carrying too much weight around the gut. Mona trembled with glee as they approached,

'Oh now I know we are going to have party boys.'

The two men, both in their early twenties shook hands vigorously,

'This is Victor; I won't try and tell you his native name.' Mona indicated the tall tattooed man, 'he is a minor chief.'

'S*** Mona, there's no need for all that stuff,' turning to the two seaman he withdrew his great fist of a hand, 'Which one are you off lads? This here is Benny,' he said jerking a thumb at his silent companion. The short stocky man just nodded.

'We are off the *Plymouth*; would you like a beer mate?' I asked.

'That's what we came for.'

Mona, grinning from ear to ear cried,

'Let's have a party at my place; Saturday night would not be right without knees up.

The three young women had at this stage just stood looking nervously around the place as if to see if the cops were present. My eyes wandered over the face and form of a small, almost diminutive girl with sparkling black eyes and a figure of perfect proportions showed off by a clinging, but plain cotton dress of a deep burnt orange colour; her black hair cut short in the current elfin Audrey Hepburn style.

'What about you girls then?' Ron asked.

'Just three shandies for them, 'Mona was quick to reply, 'Meet Terri, Sue and Laurie.'

We moved from the bar to an adjacent table. Terri turned out to be the neat little one that I had sensed just might be a little interested in me too. Victor told a few quick jokes which had Ron going in return. Much laughter and many beers later, just before the dreaded six o' clock closing time, in marched Billy Pitt.

'Right oh you lot what's going on?'

'We are about to purchase a few bottles and adjourn to Mona's place for a bit of a do, I shall enquire if we would be permitted to invite a great ugly bastard like you.' Turning to the group Ron stated, 'This person is our ship's cook, do we require his presence do you think?'

'Oh yes please,' Laurie cooed.

Bill stared at the company with his miss matched eyes taking in the silent thug like figure of Benny and the mass of tattooed Victor, he eyed the bulk of Mona and his gaze did not miss the charms of the three ladies. The pause was momentary, 'You had better count me in or there will be short rations for the two of you.'

We all purchased several bottles of Dominion Bitter and headed over the railway tracks to Mona's place. Mona and Benny were obviously a couple, and another tall fine-featured Maori woman who greeted us at the door, was married to Victor. That left the three girls suspiciously convenient for the trio of merry sailors.

In the small brick house, surrounded by neat garden beds, noticeably clean and comfortable, Billy relaxed. Both of us had suspected a set up for drunken lads ashore. Lamb chops were thrown on a barbeque and Mary Jane, Vic's wife made salads; Pat Boone started to croon about 'Love letters in the Sand', and Tom realised these were genuinely friendly people who liked to entertain. The atmosphere became convivial and increasingly raucous.

Terri and I smooched around a bit and then went into the back yard for a smoke.

Terri, actually turned out to be a nickname for Theresa Barsac, her father a French sailor attached to a British ship during WWII, and her mother, who was part Maori and part Welsh, lived in Auckland on the north shore. The father had never returned to New Zealand, missing out on knowing this exotic little beauty. Because she was not quite eighteen, the age for legal drinking in hotels, the nervous looks in the pub were explained; in a small town, everyone knows everyone, especially the cops.

We danced some more, and around ten p.m., Mona, by this time well liquored up decided it was time for her party trick. Victor and Benny rolled their eyes in dismay, but she told them to bring two kitchen chairs and place them in the middle of the room. This they reluctantly did and stood back with folded arms to watch the fun and games.

Mona pointed at our Ron and told him to place his head and shoulders on one chair, and his feet minus his shoes on the other. Always ready for a laugh Ronnie complied without a qualm. Next, she leaned over his face waving a green charm on a silver chain in a pendulum like manner before his startled eyes.

'Do not take your eyes off this magic stone; it goes back to a time before the white man came. Watch; watch it closely, you will feel your body rise up, weightless. Watch; close your mind to all else.'

Vic moved quietly to the chair supporting Ron's feet.

'When I say 'Rangitofua' you will rise up, don't worry just watch the stone of peace?'

Suddenly she cried out 'Rangitofua'! Vic pulled the chair from beneath his feet and Ron fell in a heap to the roars of bottled up laughter from the audience who had stifled their giggles during the performance the crumpled victim joined in with a good-natured yell of, 'Never mind better luck next time, as the actress said to the bishop.'

Mona looked downcast,

'One of these days I'll get it right, you see if I don't, my gran could do it she had the power.'

'Yeah, but she didn't guzzle beer all day,' put in Mary-Jane, 'maybe her concentration was pure and unimpaired.'

The dancing began again, but very soon, it was time for the girls to head back to Christchurch their home base, a taxi was ordered just in time to catch the last train.

'Will I see you again?' I asked as I gave and received a goodnight kiss.

'Phone me at home tomorrow here is the number; don't call too early though if you wake my brother who's a night club waiter he will be unbearable all day.'

In the evening of the following day Terri and I went to the cinema, after which she told me that she had to return to her home in Auckland her holiday in Christchurch over. We agreed to meet there when my ship arrived in that city in a week or two. I tucked her phone number away very carefully. We sailed back to Wellington, then on to Napier, and finally Auckland.

Whilst in Napier, Billy Ron and I had a run in with the local constabulary. After a few quick beers, we were returning to the ship at around 6:15pm on a glorious summer evening. Our journey took us through a beachside park, with an ornamental shell shaped public bandstand. Ronnie decided he needed to urinate so with no toilets nearby; he went behind a screen of bushes. However, he was not sufficiently hidden from a bunch of passing schoolgirls, who commenced to yell blue murder. A pair of patrolling constables heard their screams and came hot foot to the rescue. We took off at a rapid rate of knots. Billy and I clambered up onto the roof of a shed, and lay low. Silly Ron just kept on running, and naturally was caught. We distinctly heard one of the "coppers" say he was going to be charged with indecent exposure. We were not about to have that, so jumping down from our place of concealment we challenged the young constables to prove it.

'If you two don't move along you'll be in for a charge too.'

'You can't do this,' Billy cried in protest, 'he was only taking a leek.'

'There are public toilets at the back of the stage, he should have gone there.'

'We didn't see 'em,' I yelled.

One of the guardians of law and order grabbed me by the arm.

'Right you're coming with us son.'

'The hell I am,' and with that I shrugged off the restraining arm and gave him a shove. Out came the handcuffs and all three of us were marched off to the 'nick'.

Next morning up before the magistrate, Billy saved Ron from the serious offence, of which he was charged, by asking a pertinent question. 'In which direction was the offender looking at the time of this alleged obscene exposure?' All witnesses had to admit that it was away from the direction of the girls.

We were still fined a 'fiver' each for resisting arrest, and I copped another three 'quid' for obstructing a policeman in the course of his duty. The skipper took another day's pay off us, and I have to say that was the most expensive piss of all time.

Auckland being the northern most of the cities in this fair land has a temperate climate. The docks are virtually at the foot of the main street, which is called Queen Street, this is, or was, the hub of activity in the early 'sixties. This thoroughfare lined on either side with shops, cafés, hotels and a cinema, rises gently in a straight line from the wharves. The late afternoon sun spread shadows across the pavements as Bill and I, with Ron tagging along as usual, strolled out to explore, after work.

Once again, the iniquitous six p.m. closing of the hotel bars caused us to slake our thirst in a hurry. The hotel we chose was called not very originally "The Auckland". Our choice was providential, as it seemed to be the favourite "watering hole" of seamen working on the Kiwi coast. This became our headquarters during our lengthy stop over for homeward bound cargo. Amongst our new acquaintances were a number of men who had "jumped" ship, (deserted), most of whom enjoyed a well-paid job and had settled down with a wife and children. I became extremely envious, firstly of their courage to take the chance of a new life, also the money they earned. Some were on the coastal shipping, others on the new harbour bridge just then under construction, which would eventually connect the city with commuters from the north shore suburbs which is where most of the beachside communities were to be found. Others worked "up bush", and came into town very rarely.

Terri and I made it our rendezvous after work, went to the weekly dance at the Polynesian Club, or the movies, or just hung out at her mother's house. The passion of our romance grew and grew. Terri's mother and young sister made me more than welcome; so much so that when the day of our departure finally arrived, there was no way I could say farewell. In the still of night I packed a small suitcase leaving most of my gear aboard, the gangway head was clear; looking as nonchalant as possible and keeping to the deeper shadows, I walked to the bus station and into a new life.

At first I got odd jobs, one at the abattoir which made me puke and lasted less than an hour, and another putting baked beans and spaghetti into tins. Eventually the other "jumpers" convinced me that to make money and also hide from the police the best thing was to head for the bush for at least six months. Toward this end I found myself on a ramshackle old Bedford bus that rattled through the cold black night carrying me to the north island hinterland away from the possibility of being nabbed by the infamous Detective Sergeant Dicky Bird, the terror of all ship "jumpers". A chief steward on Union Steam had promised to help me get a ship on my return. This was purely a speculative journey with no guarantee of a job at the lumber mill the guys had told me about. All I knew was that they often needed unskilled labour. Fortunately, on the bus I made the acquaintance of a man who had worked at the mill for a number of years, he filled me in on all the dos and don'ts and as the bus arrived late in the evening he let me spend the night on his living room couch. This act is typical of the generosity of all the people I met In New Zealand back then. Next day he drove me to the mill and took me to the personnel officer. Within the hour I had a job on the maintenance crew, had dumped my suitcase in a tiny hut with two bunks and a wood stove heater and reported to the foreman. Amazingly no questions were asked as to my identity and I filled in a tax form in the name of Tom Collier. The wage was really good, after tax and rent for the hut, a token two shillings and sixpence and three pounds five shillings for three meals a day in the canteen, the remainder was saved. The back woods hut was a classic, right out of an adventure story. Built for two men to share it had two bunks with a thin straw filled palliasse and a wood stove for winter warmth. That was it; no cupboards, no wardrobe, no sink for a wash, all ablutions were carried out at a large central building that also housed the kitchens and canteen. The food was amazing; for breakfast there were eggs, as many as one could eat, chops, bacon, steak, baked beans, grilled tomatoes, cereals and toast. For lunch we were handed a pack of enormous sandwiches, slabs of cake, and fruit, which we ate on the job.

The air was clean and crisp, the scenery breathtaking, and the work sufficient to build up young muscles, but not too tedious. All the men I worked with were helpful and as I was in the maintenance crew there was plenty of overtime. The only draw back was my lonely little wooden hut. I sorely missed my shipmates and of course the stunning Miss Barsac. The Kinleith Mill is, or was a huge conglomeration of sheds and towers, the timber came into the yards in huge trucks, when off loaded it was cut into wood products of all kinds.

Saturday afternoon at the local pub was an education. The vast majority of the drinkers came from the mill, and most of them were either "drifters", or "jumpers" like me, or legitimate migrants seeking that which could not be found in the country of their birth; all lonely hard drinking men, toughened by life in the forests, generous to a fault with friends, however deadly dangerous to their enemies. Fights between rival groups were commonplace. Broadly speaking we had Maoris and Islanders, who kept to themselves, the Brits, the Europeans, German, Dutch, Polish, Slavs; laughter would echo as the jokes flew; off course betting on the horse races broadcast over the radio would eat up a lot of their pay, the odds provided by a S.P. bookmaker. My little group of ex-seamen seemed to congregate as if a magnet drew us together. We talked of ships and far away places. New Zealand was to become to us a home, a dream come true. Nothing marred our horizons; we had escaped from the grim European winters, filthy streets, and narrow parochial minds. The whole of the Southern Seas, the new, new world was ours.

Then fate stepped in. After several months of lonely nights and hard work, I decided to go into Auckland for a weekend. Of course I should have seen it coming. My lovely Terri with temptation on the doorstep in the form of an American cruiser in port, and with no knowledge of my arrival, was dating a rating of the cruiser. She told me in no uncertain terms my presence was not required. Over the years, these "damn yanks" had become a thorn in our collective sides. They had more money than sense and threw it around like confetti. I had never been angrier in my life. Always on a short fuse, I gave her a very nasty mouthful of abuse and stormed out of the inner city house she was using to meet her "Yankee" Lothario; if I could have found him he'd have got the same, with a knuckle sandwich to go with it.

Slamming out the door I headed straight for the Auckland Hotel. Disaster struck a few hundred yards down the road, dressed in my London tailored suit, a smart double breasted in black barathea, I stuck out like a spare bride at a wedding. Walking and trying to calm myself I paused to look in a shop window. I saw the reflected image of a police car draw to the curb. Two young 'coppers' stepped out and headed straight for me. 'Well now if it isn't the dashing young Mr Morgan,' one of them slyly remarked. Quick as a flash I said,

'You've got the wrong bloke mate.'

'Oh, and so who are you?'

116

'Colliers the name sport,' I bluffed, 'just in from Tokaroa for the weekend.'

'So that's where you've been hiding is it?'

'Hiding, why would I be hiding, and whom from?'

'Give it up Morgan; you don't remember me do you? You're the young tearaway seaman from the *Plymouth* that shoved me in Napier, and that suit is a dead give away, they don't cut them like that in Auckland You're arrested for illegal entry into New Zealand. You should have stayed in Tokaroa.'

At least detective sergeant 'Dicky' Bird was pleased to see me.

'You are one unlucky lad,' he said as I was pushed into his scruffy little office on Princes pier, 'the warrant for your arrest was posted in Napier, I've never heard of you.'

Dickie was pleasant enough, a roly-poly sort of man with a balding dome and a happy countenance, he added with a chuckle,

'You will have to spend a few days at our expense in Mount Crawford jail, never mind, you get three square meals a day and we will send you home to your mum free of charge.'

'Ha ha,' was all I could think of to say, in my dejected state of mind.

It was over, the dream had ended, all because that "berk" Ron had pissed in the wrong place. I hoped I'd catch up with him again some day; I thought very dark thoughts about both him and Terri.

Finger printed, photographed, and bundled into the back of a "paddy wagon", we set off. No seats in the wagon, just a cold metal deck, and bugger all to hang on to as the driver deliberately took the corners too sharply. I was all alone in the vehicle still in my beautifully tailored suit which by now was looking the worse for wear. My state of mind wandered from sanguine to down right angry for not staying put in Tokaroa. Finally the shame of prison hit me like a physical blow. This wonderful adventure, my brave new world reduced to degradation, my pride slowly crumbled me into a dejected heap.

By the time I was ushered into the grim, grey, dank, dark interior of Mount Crawford, the ego had reduced to the size of a peanut. I stood with two or three other men; I did not raise my head to look around, just stared at the concrete floor. Belt, tie, shoelaces, contents of pockets, all taken away, and coarse prison garb thrust into my arms. Soap, towel, blanket, pillow, stacked on top of the grey uniform.

'Strip off, take a shower, put on your nice new gear, 'a surly officer snarled.

The showers, all in one long dimly lit room, had no provision for privacy, no partitions; glancing up I saw my companions, one big Maori, the other two, old blokes, who looked as grey as the walls in their nakedness. Not a word was exchanged between us; apart from the grunts as the tepid water hit our shivering bodies. We got back into our own underwear, put on the rough uniform, and marched off to our remand cells.

Gratefully, I was pleased to find that my eight feet square cell had a single cot. I would be alone in my misery. The whitewashed walls and concrete floor were clean; the small cot had a thin mattress just like the one in my hut at Tokaroa. Folding Mr Krett's outstanding, (give away), suit carefully; I laid it on the floor as there was no wardrobe, not even a hook or a ruddy nail.

For ten days, I mopped floors, and walked in a yard full of silent shuffling men. I washed in a trough, and shaved under supervision, with a blunt razor blade, (fortunately my beard is light), rough red Lifebuoy soap and cold water. Grey, everything was grey; towering walls casting grim shadows, a place with no joy or laughter, the sun rarely seen except as a golden glow in a patch of blue once a day for a few minutes. The lonely early nights in Trinidad were as nothing compared to this comfortless, soul destroying agony of mind.

The day of my trial dawned with pouring rain rattling off the cab of the police car, as we made the short journey down town. They must have decided I was the most docile of prisoners, no handcuffs; I even scored a smile from my escort.

I stood in the dock, grubby shirt, creased suit, defeated attitude. I raised my eyes and surveyed the courtroom. Terri and her mother sat on the very front of the polished wooden benches, staring up at me, neither smiled. I agreed with every echoing word as the charge was read out, pleaded guilty, and prayed silently for a ship to carry me home.

'We will grant bail until such time as a vessel can repatriate this man.'

Terri's mother stood up and faced the magistrate,

'I'll stand bond for this man your honour sir,' she quavered.

Outside the courthouse, after the paperwork got done, I stood blinking in the sunshine that followed the rain. The golden glow of the rain washed streets offered a new beginning. I resolved to quell my impetuous nature and whilst offering my profuse thanks listened gratefully as the dear lady also offered me her home until a suitable ship was found to take me home. I gently refused, Terri stood silently at her side.

'Thanks just the same Mrs Barsac, I have saved a few pounds and shall find some lodgings and possibly a job while I wait, thank you for the posting of the bail, I won't let you down.'

Turning to the silent and oh so lovely daughter I gave her a sad smile, the bitter regret burning my throat. 'It won't work now Terri, all my naive romantic notions about us have been well and truly scuppered, I could never trust you. I am a seaman and on the oceans of the world I will always be wondering what you are up to, take care of your mother and yourself, because I doubt those b***** American sailors will.'

I returned to Tokaroa and regretfully gathered up my gear, bade farewell to pastoral paradise and climbed aboard the ramshackle bus to the city. I found lodgings in a suburb of Wellington close to the construction site of the mighty bridge being built to span the bay. Most of the men staying at the boarding house worked in one capacity or another on the bridge, one, a foreman of the machine shop, on hearing of my Tokaroa work gave me a job as a fitters mate. I fetched and carried, got thoroughly dirty and enjoyed every minute of it. I drank beer with the high flying steel riggers and with divers working in caissons on the harbour bed. With my savings from the mill, plus the wage from The Cleveland and Ohio Bridge Co., I soon had over one hundred NZ pounds in the bank. Once a week I reported to the local cop shop and also the Harbour Master's office. No vacancies for stewards. Sergeant Dickie Bird stuck his oar in with a comment about putting me on the first passenger liner leaving for the UK as a supernumerary.

One day as I walked with my new mates off the bridge site one of the riggers, a little nuggety scouser said, 'Ya know if I was you Morg, I'd do a ringbolt across to Aussie.'

'What's a ringbolt mate?' I asked.

'Well keep it under your hat mate, but if you get yourself down to Wellington and go to a certain pub where the lads on the Oz ferry drink, they'll sneak you aboard and you walk ashore in Sydney, no worries, no passport no questions asked, get me?'

I got him alright, this was the break I'd been waiting for; I gave a weeks notice and with four clear days before I had to report again, jumped on the train. It was so easy I wondered at the immigration department's slackness, however back then it was the innocent years of the early 60s. A few beers with the lads off the ferry and I walked on like one of the crew. So much for curbing my impetuosity. For the crossing of about forty eight hours I slept on the deck of one of the crew cabins and wandered around like a passenger. In Sydney I wandered off with my well travelled suitcase, the old portable Imperial was long gone, at Piermont quay and found lodgings near Kings Cross for two nights then caught a train for Melbourne.

The word was that although the Snowy Mountain hydro electric scheme was almost finished, there was still work to be had. It seemed ideal; the scheme was swarming with "New Australians" where I could lose myself in a crowd. Anonymity was the key. Khancoban was swarming with "Poms" or so I was told. The bus took me there via Albury and I ended up 'slinging hash' in the kitchens. Tom Johnson seemed a good enough name to sign on with and that is what the tax department forms read. Labouring in the shadow of Mount Kosciusko, I was once again in big skies and clean air. In the kitchens I sweated in hot in summer and enjoyed cosy warmth in the high country winter. My chums in the bunk house gave me cigarettes for extra portions of grub. I stuck it for a year, my hundred pounds had more than doubled and I felt safe enough to head south again. The men at the Snowy were just as rough and ready as the fellows in the Kin Leith mill. When the leaves of autumn coloured the rugged terrain and the first nip of winter chilled the crystal clear air, accompanied by two Italian migrants I headed out in a Holden utility with our swags in the back. We were a trio of itinerate workers enjoying life and ready for anything.

We tried fruit picking around Shepparton for a while, sharing the caravan with the guys from the Snowy. I tried to teach them English and they taught me the love of Tuscan cooking and homemade vino. We spent sun filled days among the fruit trees and riotous nights chasing 'Sheilas', around the camp site. It couldn't last of course.

The three of us went into town on a Saturday afternoon to put a bet on a horse race and have a few beers; my last two birthdays had passed by and with scarcely a thought and here I was aged twenty one with another birthday on the horizon. We found the SP bookie in the usual pub and ordered our beers. The barmaid laughed at the accent of one of my friends, and asked where we were from. As I explained a voice from a corner of the long bar said in a loud stage whisper, 'Goodness, mate will you look at that lot, a Pom and two wogs, what this place is coming to?' Most Aussies I had met would say words of that kind laughingly, but not this bloke. He stood with half a dozen rough looking bastards in overalls and blue singlets, their boots caked with red mud. My friends, whom I called Sal for Salvadore and Big Joe for Giuseppe, had been in the Snowy for five or six years and were as tough as the mountains they had dug through. They knew trouble when it was brewing like a winter storm over Kosciusko.

This was the last thing I needed, my low profile out the window for sure. Sal pushed himself off the bar and turned his thick strong body toward the gang. He was short, maybe five and a half feet, with no waist and shoulders as wide as he was tall. His short cropped premature balding head sat on a neck as thick as a blue gum stump. 'What's wrong mister, you donna like see peoples enjoy a quiet beer?' He turned to Joe whom was a foot taller and just as big, 'put da money in a da pock Joe and we go.' Joe scooped up his change, and rattled it in his fist.

'What for we gotta go Tommy gotta shout yet?'

We moved toward the door and wouldn't you know big mouth had to make one last smart remark. 'F*****' wogs, dagos and b***** pommies are taking over the b***** country.'

The change was still in Joe's hand, he hurled it at this mob and it flew like pellets. 'That's all your b***** country worth big mouth,' and it was on. Sal and Joe cut through this bunch like enraged bulls on the run. Two of them were down before you could say "s***"; I followed and gave the "mouth" a kick in the balls with my size ten work boots, and Joe held one dumb looking red faced character by the neck shaking him like a rag doll. That was it, it was all over in seconds, the remaining heroes were out the door, with Sal giving them loud verbals in picturesque Italian. The bookmaker came over and said,

'Youse blokes had better shove off before the law gets here the landlord has rung the coppers.'

The "mouth" lay on the floor in an agonised ball; the other three had struggled upright and leaned heavily on the bar for support. Tables and chairs lay scattered in pools of beer, the innkeeper screaming,

'Out, out, get out you pack o'bastards!'

'Come on you two let's leg it fast,' I yelled!

Sal wanted to stay, 'What for we gotta run?' not an unreasonable question since we had not started it however the law was not what I needed, at any time, never mind now. 'Please trust me and get in the car Sal, the coppers here are not friendly.' So we scarpered back to camp whilst listening on the radio to our horse win at Flemington at three to one.

My friends could not understand why I had to go to Melbourne and fast, so I explained that if the coppers came asking questions I was in deep s***.

'No worries Tommy, I gotta cousin in Melbourne, lives in Reservoir, you go see him, I'll phone and let him know you coming OK?'

My life has been filled with men like Sal and Joe, the fellows in Port of Spain, those on the bridge and in the timber camp, crews on ships, and never have they ever shown a mean spirit. If you are open in your manner, enjoy a good laugh, pay your debts and always remember when to "shout" a round of drinks, you will be accepted, until such time as you f*** up.

In the 'Snowy' I had filled out a tax form and had received a file number and that was the number I gave to Mario, Sal's cousin, when I started work as a waiter in his suburban restaurant. With my black hair and brown eyes, plus a deep sun tan I looked the very epitome of your suave Latin except when I opened my mouth. I deliberately led the customers on with a cheeky smile and the smattering I had picked up from Sal and Joe, and then explained the menu in perfect English. It worked well and the tips were generous. I lived rent free in a cement sheet sleep-out at the back of Mario's weatherboard home and went by tram to Carlton where the bistro style restaurant provided me with good money and excellent food.

For the first time in years I felt secure enough to write home to my family and reassure them that all was well. I had a permanent address; I wrote home and return mail came often, much to my delight. My pesky cousin had married and moved to Essex and my aunt had moved to her own flat. My mother and sister had a cosy top floor apartment courtesy of the local council.

I worked a six day week in what they call split shifts, first lunch twelve until three, and then a break of two hours until dinner, in those two hours I explored Melbourne. More often than not one of the quaint old green trams without doors, only canvas flaps to let down in the rain, took me to Princes Pier where I watched ships docking or sailing. Passengers disembarked from ocean liners that brought thousands of migrants seeking a new life. This passenger terminal lay adjacent to a sandy strip of beach and I would sit contentedly watching the waves advance and retreat whilst keeping a weather eye open for the shipping that flowed daily down Port Phillip Bay. It was on one such day I saw the familiar red funnel and grey hull of a Port Line vessel. My heart jumped into my mouth, could it possibly be? No surely not; the coincidence too much to hope for. However as she approached the terminal she stayed on course and did not head off for Webb Dock where the commercial cargoes unloaded.

That heart stopping night that I had walked off the *Plymouth* in Auckland seemed an age ago, yet it was just short of two years. Would this be her and if so was Billy Pitt still rustling grub for crew and passengers? The clean lines certainly looked like her, the bow sliced easily through the calm waters. Nearer and nearer she came and yes it was the ship that had carried me into this life of adventure. I wanted to be on the wharf waving and calling but I knew this would be folly; the officers that remained would spot me and report me and run to old Nielsen. I walked across to the Seaman's Mission and phoned the shipping agents asking if a phone number had been allocated to the *Plymouth,* yes it was a regular line allotted to that berth. I watched from a safe distance until *Plymouth* had secured all lines and the gangway had been swayed down. From experience I knew the phone was one of the first items aboard, I dialled and asked in my best Aussie accent for Bill Pitt.

'Hang on mate I'll get him,' was the response. You beauty I thought my old mate is still aboard. After a long wait Bill's Cockney accent filled my ear.

'Who's this?' he asked.

I gripped the phone tight and prayed, 'Billy it's Morg, Tommy, how you doing you old sea cook?' I yelled with excitement.

'My goodness! Morg are you in Melbourne?'

'You'd better believe it my son.'

'What the heck are you doing in Melbourne?'

'It's a long story old mate, meet me for a beer after lunch tomorrow and I'll tell you all about it. Obviously I can't be seen near the docks so you'll have to come up town. Do you know the London Tavern in Elizabeth Street?'

The London was a lovely old pub with a long bar on the ground floor and hotel lounge up above. Middle aged barmaids served at various stations along the mahogany length. It was a happy, atmospheric watering hole very popular with city workers. At four o clock on the afternoon after *Plymouth* docked I waited impatiently for my old friend watching the main entrance, the smoky room began to fill with thirsty workers jostling for a place at the bar. Another fifteen minutes passed and I began to feel anxious, suddenly a hand clapped me on the shoulder from behind, I reckon I jumped three feet in the air; I turned ready to run if it was the law.

Of course it was Billy and standing next to him with a grin as big as Texas stood Mac. 'You sneaky bastards how did you get in the place without me seeing you and how in hell did you get to be here Mac?' My hand was crushed in Mac's mighty paw and much back thumping ensued.

'I've been in this pub more times than you've had hot dinners my son,' cried Bill, 'there's a back entry into the lane, caught you; I bet you've got skid marks in your knickers. Explain yourself Mac before the ship jumping rat bursts a boiler.'

'Well it's pretty easy really, I got the letter you sent to my home saying you were with Port Line and on the *Plymouth* so I went down to the shore side super's office and asked when she was due back and then hung around at home. The day she docked I was first up the gangway only to find you had skipped in Kiwiland. I signed on anyway, and we did an eight month trip to NZ. I worked by the coast back home and nearly baled out when I heard she was headed for Oz next trip, I'm glad I didn't now. In the meantime I'd met Billy over a beer or three and talking over old voyages we discovered our mutual acquaintance was a "pillock" called Tommy Morgan.'

We moved away from the by now crowded bar, and I told them my full story, and then confided, 'to be honest fellas, I'm sick of being on the run. I feel safe enough here but if I ever wanted to go home there's no way without going back into the "nick" for a while. My boss is the only one who knows the full story and he will keep quiet only as long as I tow the line.'

'Listen mate,' said Mac concern written all over his sun tanned face, 'Billy knows a few people here and we are going to a ball at the town hall on Saturday night, you had better come along and meet a few people. Relax and enjoy yourself you might meet someone.'

'A b***** ball, what you two, you've gotta be joking.'

'No mate it's true, Bill knows these girls whom work for the TAA airline and they have invited him and me to their annual bash; they said we could bring along two more blokes.'

'I'm working Saturday night. I finish at around ten, it's only ten minutes in a taxi I could meet you there.'

'It's a deal, now let's get stuck into a few, it's great to see you again you silly bastard. Your dick has led you into more strife than this Aussie robber bloke Ned Kelly,' said Bill.

I was late back on the job that evening but all was well, and Saturday night I conned the other waiter into finishing off for me, serving the deserts and coffee. I changed in the back room and cabbed it to the town hall on the corner of Collins and Swanston. My name was at the door and I was given a table number to find and there they were, well oiled as usual with three gorgeous girls. A six piece band led by a not so good sax player was churning out a foxtrot as I sat down. After intros all round Bill poured me a warm beer from a jug. 'Let me get a fresh one of those,' I muttered looking for a waiter. Just then a man I did not know approached the table with a stunning blonde on his arm.

'Oi you lot, where's the cold beer, it's hot work out there, who's this then?' he asked looking at me through bloodshot eyes. I could see he was drunk and the lass on his arm embarrassed. 'This is an old mate of ours Jim,' Mac replied, 'meet Tom.' I noticed he deliberately left my last name off, and I got the hint not to trust Jim.

The blonde sat down and fiddled with a spoon left on the table cloth after the meal had been served, she had long slim fingers with no rings. I waited for someone to do the honours; obviously Jim had bad manners to go with the drunken leers he gave the lass.

'Hi,' I said, she raised amazing emerald green eyes, a tiny smile twitched in the corner of a delicious mouth that sat under a straight nose which set off a heart shaped face. My chest heaved and gulping air I reached across to shake her hand, 'I'm Jan,' she said.

The waiter hovered, I called for a fresh jug and the girls all had brandy crusters. The band jumped into a bracket of up tempo swing, I asked Jan for a dance, and we swung easily into a jive.

Arriving back at the table under the baleful glare of Jim we sat side by side. On learning that I lived in Reservoir, Jan informed me that she lived close by in Preston. By this time Jim had had two more beers and was almost legless, he was a steward off the boat and one of the blind dates set up by Billy. In the toilet Mac informed me that it would be best to say nothing to Jim about my past on the *Plymouth* as most of the crew were still from my time aboard. The skipper and chief steward would all remember me if word got out. We arrived back in time for the last bracket of waltzes, Jim the idiot was asleep with his head on the table; Jan cocked a bright green gaze in my direction, I gestured to the dance floor and she nodded. When it was all over Mac and Bill carried the dozy Jim to the cab rank, and Jan and I hopped into another and headed north. Jan Nichols lived in a neat weatherboard off Bell Street, and I deposited her there with a phone number snug in my wallet.

The next day being a Sunday I rang to see if she would like to see a movie, she said she would, and we jumped on a tram into the city and went to the Regent. I told her I was an immigrant and all about the Snowy and fruit picking, she in turn told me about the eighteen years of her life with her mother, step father and sister and her job at TAA.

On Monday night Billy and Mac came to the restaurant for dinner, when all was quiet we sat with a bottle of vino. Mario like his cousin was a kind and generous man; he gave me the keys telling me to help myself to another bottle and left us to our reminiscences. Feeling mellow with wine I blurted out,

'You know something fellas, I envy you sailing off soon, and I've totally messed up. I have no home, no passport, and I can't even get a driving licence. What happens if there is trouble of some kind at home, how the hell can I buy a ticket; I live with a false identity?'

Billy as always came up with the answer,

'You have always been a game bugger, what about stowing away again.'

'What are you crazy? Old Nielsen will hang me from the b***** yardarm.'

'Now just listen, despite being an idiot you're a British national, and what's more you are known on board. Since I got the chief cook's job I have a big cabin and bathroom plus certain privileges, if we can get you aboard under cover of darkness the night before we sail for home you can hide in my cabin for two or three days then give yourself up. Nielsen won't turn back as we are homeward bound.'

Mac chimed in with, 'It might just work Tom, you know everyone aboard and they know you're a good worker, just a little cunt struck that's all. When we get home you will have trouble with immigration, but what did you do in the UK - nothing. Port Line will be pissed off, but again what can they do, except return your discharge book with a bad report. You will be home and whatever the consequences you're big enough and ugly enough to take it. What have you got to lose Tom my son, you can't stay in limbo for the rest of your life?'

They were right, the risk being that if I got caught before the ship sailed then I would be in Pentridge for sure, however they would still repatriate me after a while. Then I thought of Jan; we had shared a brief kiss or two but somehow I just felt she was *The One*. My stomach felt sour, my brain spun in circles, what to do, what to do? There was week to go before decision time, 'I'll let you know in a couple of days, all right?'

On Wednesday night Jan came into the restaurant with her sister Josie who was a lively, attractive, about to be married girl of my own age. As if some nod of approval had been given by big sister Jan agreed to come back to my humble sleep out at the back of Mario's. Our love making was fast and furious, and far from satisfying. I was tempted to tell her of my dilemma; to stay or go, however I said nothing except I'd see her again on Sunday.

The next two days were a nightmare as I agonised over the situation. At work I was distracted enough for Mario to reprimand me several times until on Friday as we were closing up he asked, 'Hey Tommy what's the problem, you sick, you in love, what?'

I had to talk to somebody, and as we sat in the gloom, the smell of garlic heavy in the air, I unburdened my soul. Mario opened a bottle of Italian Chianti and poured us each a brimming glass, his handsome head with its mop of thick black hair nodded in sympathy, 'I also get homesick Tommy, I think of Tuscany and I could weep,' his expressive brown eyes did in fact look as if they would shed tears, 'you know there is nowhere in the world as beautiful, but there is no work, the people are poor so we come here to a new life. Melbourne is dreary but OK it will get better. Six o' clock closing is a joke, the whole place is shut down by ten, and Sunday is more religious here than in Rome. We Italians all treasure family life so we make our own enjoyment, but for you I see the problem, loneliness yes, but now you have a beautiful girlfriend, how can you make a family if you are a phantom? No name to give the bambinos.'

This last was stated with a smile and as he topped up our glasses. 'You are right how can I get married? I have no birth certificate anything, I just have to go home Mario and sort all this out.' He idly brushed a few crumbs off the table, 'What I do now if you go, customers like you, my wife like you, mate you can make a good Aussie?'

'You know I like it here Mario and yes, Jan and I could make a go of it. I will come back only this time as the real me, so tomorrow will be last day here mate, if you see Sal and Joe give them my best.'

Sunday was a difficult time, I dared not tell Jan of my plans for fear of gossip. We walked around Melbourne's glorious Botanical Gardens, the weather was kind and we sat in the shade of a massive oak tree in warm sunshine. I wanted to say goodbye at her front gate but her mother came out, 'Why don't you bring your friend in Jan?'

An uncomfortable hour was spent filling them in on the life and times of Tom Johnson and I walked out of there thanking my lucky stars it would be the last time I would have to prevaricate. There was nothing in my room that I needed other than the clothes on my back plus my razor and tooth brush. I had no bank account to empty however a decent roll of notes nestled in my pocket. Dressed in my only suit I made my way to the Seaman's Mission opposite Princes Pier. It was dark and past eight pm when I arrived, Bill was waiting at the gate. *Plymouth* had sailed around from Webb dock that afternoon to pick up the usual ten or twelve passengers on the pier.

'All hands are on watch already Tom, and that includes Mac, so why don't we go for a stroll down to Saint Kilda for a coffee, by the time we get back all should be quiet aboard.' And so it was, there was not a soul at the gangway head where a small blackboard announced sailing time as 0630 next morning. Watch keepers were busy or sleeping, the catering staff was either in the passenger quarters or catching up on sleep. We slipped quietly into Bill's cabin totally unnoticed; I began to breathe a little easier. My bed was to be a leather couch beneath the porthole, a bit short for my six foot frame but it would do. Bill locked the door, and turning to me said,

'If anyone knocks on the door head for the bathroom, I'm going up to the galley to see if all is under control, my second cook is alright but I have to check. Then I'll go to the mess for cocoa as usual, probably play a game of darts or crib, best to look normal mate; lock the door behind me and only open for my voice.'

The next forty eight hours were the longest and most nerve racking of my life; Billy managed to keep all hands away from his cabin and brought me a meal or two. However on Wednesday morning I knew it was all over because with captain's rounds due at 1030 hours either Nielsen or the chief mate would look into every cabin. Elegant Evans came into the cabin with a stern faced Bill a little after breakfast had been served.

'Morgan,' he cried 'what sort of a cock up do you call this?' In a strange way I was pleased to be called by my real name.

'I'm sorry boss, but this was the only way I could see to get myself sorted out.'

'Yeah, your mate here, whom you have got into a cart load of trouble, has told me the full story. So now it's up to the bridge with you my son.'

On the way along alleyways and up companion ways we received a great many startled looks until finally arriving on the bridge where Captain Nielsen stood fairly bursting with rage. His big moon face normally kindly was purple. 'How dare you? Morgan you're an imbecile. Do you realise the enormity of this folly?' He fulminated and stamped about the bridge, the duty apprentice midshipman escaped to the wing, the helmsman stared stoically ahead, the third mate glowered and Evans shifted his feet nervously.

'Both you and William Pitt shall pay for this, I'll have you drummed out of the fleet and Morgan I'll see to it that you never go to sea again. Now get out of my sight. Mr Evans kindly bring that other fool Pitt up here immediately.'

When Bill returned from the bridge he found me in the cooks' and stewards mess drinking tea. 'Well that's that matey you've got a free trip home, he logged me a weeks pay and no doubt I'll get a bollocking from the super when we get home, but I doubt I'll lose my job. I've been aboard this ship since her maiden voyage and it's the first time I've put a foot wrong. Skipper reckons immigration will go bananas but as you are a British national they'll more than likely ground you without a discharge book and getting a passport may be difficult for a while.'

Spiritually buoyed, I spent the next three and a half weeks washing down bulkheads and decks; I slept in the sick bay and lay on deck getting a great sun tan. Pay off day in the Pool of London immigration gave me a thorough going over; however there was no doubt as to my identity and with a parental home to go to there was no need to prosecute. The shore side catering boss came aboard with my old discharge book and eighty eight pounds and twelve shillings in pay that I had left behind in the *Plymouth* when I jumped in New Zealand, also with the grave admonition to steer well clear of Port Line forever.

Dear old Mitcham was of course unchanged, a few more dark skinned citizens bustled around the shops at Fair Green, and my mother's new flat sat atop a new high rise. Never one to be over emotional her greeting was as if I'd only been away on my holidays. The beautiful Brazilian butterfly tray sat in a prominent position on the mantel. Home was the sailor, home from the sea, for a little while anyway.

Next day I changed my Aussie money at the Midland bank and took Mum to the Cricketers Arms for lunch and told her about Jan.

'Well son if you truly feel you love the girl you had best write and tell her,' she said calmly. 'Who knows you might even settle down and give me some grand children'. So write I did and two weeks later I received an international 'phone call at our home from Jan. The essence of which was that she was pregnant. I knew I would get back to sea, many a ship was short handed in those days and with a great deal of perseverance a berth could be found even with a *"Voyage not Completed"* entry in the discharge book. Dilemma; the right thing was to marry the lass, mother agreed, so up to Australia House in the Strand I went. Migration papers completed, medical passed, a single man was welcomed with open arms. Within two months I was on a BOAC Bristol Britannia flight bound for Melbourne; this time as a legitimate person, even if it was as a "ten pound Pom." Within two weeks I was working as a barman at the famous Collingwood Football Club, courtesy of my new brother-in-law who played for the side. Our baby daughter was followed by a boy and they have been my life's delight. Mario, Joe and Sal are still great mates, and Billy Pitt lives in Perth Western Australia.

The End

Lightning Source UK Ltd.
Milton Keynes UK
UKOW01f1305120917
309042UK00001B/116/P